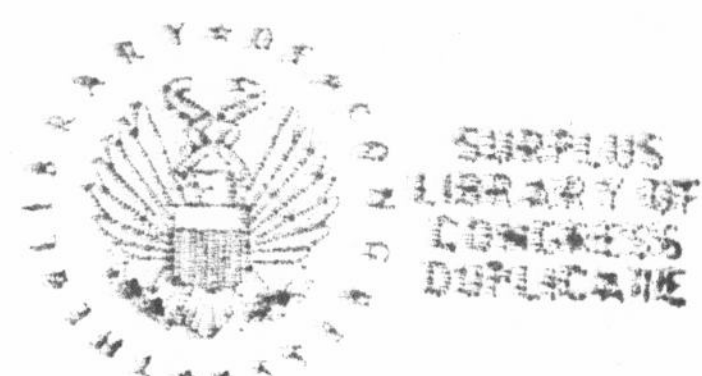
SURPLUS
LIBRARY OF
CONGRESS
DUPLICATE

RECREATION

Current Selected Research

RECREATION

Current Selected Research

Volume 1

Edited by
Fred N. Humphrey, Ph.D.
and
James H. Humphrey, Ed.D.

AMS PRESS, INC.
New York

RECREATION
Current Selected Research

ISSN 0894–4830

Series ISBN: 0–404–63900–3
Vol. 1 ISBN: 0–404–63901–1

MANUFACTURED IN THE UNITED STATES OF AMERICA

Published by
AMS Press, Inc.
56 East 13th Street
New York, N.Y. 1003

CONTENTS

Board of Reviewers

CONTRIBUTORS

M. Deborah Bialeschki, College of Arts and Sciences, The University of North Carolina, Chapel Hill, North Carolina

John O. Cooper, Department of Human Services Education, The Ohio State University, Columbus, Ohio

Michael E. Crawford, Department of Recreation and Park Administration, University of Missouri, Columbia, Missouri

F. D. Dottavio, Department of Parks, Recreation, and Tourism Management, Clemson University, Clemson, South Carolina

Mary Ellen Dugan-Jendzejec, Department of Recreation, University of Maryland, College Park, Maryland

Kathleen J. Halberg, Department of Recreation and Leisure Studies, California State University-Long Beach, Long Beach, California.

Paul Heitzenrater, Wheatridge Regional Center, Wheatridge, Colorado

Gordon E. Howard, Department of Parks, Recreation, and Tourism Management, Clemson University, Clemson, South Carolina

Karla A. Henderson, Texas Woman's University, Denton, Texas

Sandra L. Hupp, Department of Physical Education, Sport and Leisure Studies, Washington State University, Pullman, Washington

Miriam Lahey, Department of Physical Education, Recreation, and Dance, Lehman College–The City University of New York, Bronx, New York

Francis A. McGuire, Department of Parks, Recreation, and Tourism Management, Clemson University, Clemson, South Carolina

Robert W. McLellan, Department of Parks, Recreation, and Tourism Management, Clemson University, Clemson, South Carolina

Paul S. Miko, Department of Recreation and Leisure Services, Georgia Southern College, Statesboro, Georgia

Kenneth E. Mobily, Department of Leisure Studies, The University of Iowa, Iowa City, Iowa

J. T. O'Leary, National Park Service Cooperative Park Studies Unit, Clemson University, Clemson, South Carolina

Roy H. Olsson, Department of Health, Physical Education, and Leisure Services, University of South Alabama, Mobile, Alabama

Lisa C. Pesavento, Chicago State University, Chicago, Illinois

Carol Cutler Riddick, Department of Recreation, University of Maryland, College Park, Maryland

Timothy D. Schroeder, Department of Health, Physical Education, and Recreation, Northern Arizona University, Flagstaff, Arizona

Howard E. A. Tinsley, Department of Psychology, Southern Illinois University, Carbondale, Illinois

Richard S. Trafton, Department of Psychology, Southern Illinois University, Carbondale, Illinois

Allison Voight, School of Health, Physical Education, and Recreation, The Ohio State University, Columbus, Ohio

PREFACE

This first volume of *Recreation: Current Selected Research* presents original research on contemporary problems of interest to students of recreation. Invited papers investigating aspects of recreation make up this first volume.

It is the purpose of the Editors and AMS Press, Inc. to provide recreation researchers with an annual series reporting original research that investigates the issues in recreation. The volumes should support journals and annual reviews reporting on similar topics.

Recreation has evolved into a sometimes complicated and complex subject and involves, among others, biological, behavioral, and therapeutic considerations. The scholarly researchers who have contributed to this volume represent the field well, and we extend our gratitude to them for their contributions. In addition, we wish to thank the members of the board of reviewers for giving of their time and talent in evaluating the manuscripts.

A volume of this nature could serve as a basic and/or supplementary text in recreation courses. It could also serve as a reference for recreation specialists as well as others investigating similar topics.

1

THOUGHTS ON A RECONSTRUCTION OF LEISURE RESEARCH[1]

Kenneth E. Mobily

The purpose of the present paper is to suggest an approach to the reconstruction of leisure research. Several issues are essential to such a reconstruction, including the separation of objective and subjective, other ways of knowing, and questions which empiricism alone cannot answer. Regardless of how we try to measure leisure, it remains a very subjective experience. Unfortunately, efforts to quantify leisure have had a detrimental effect on other ways of knowing. Yet, the subjective and objective are not so far apart as one might initially think. The complexity of leisure suggests that we ought to attempt to know it in as many diffferent ways as possible. Rigorous inquiry is not the sole preserve of scientifically based research. Other methods can demonstrate a rigor which equals that of empirical research methods. Furthermore, empirical investigation inevitably yields an incomplete picture of leisure because it cannot address many important questions about leisure, most notably those dealing with ethics and morals. It is imperative for leisure scholars to consider methods which do in fact deal with leisure as a value-laden concept. But if methodologies remain estranged from one another, all will be guilty of explaining too little. In the end, we seek better questions to ask, better ideas to think, and richer possiblities to contemplate.

The purpose of this dialogue is to arrive at a *reasonable* judgment regarding the future direction of leisure research. Two conditions utilized by act theorists will be employed in reaching this judgment. First of all, one must know the relevent facts bearing on the problem at hand. Secondly, "you must check to make sure that you are not abnormal" (Rosen, 1978, p. 155). The major portion of this presentation will attempt to ascertain the relevant facts, but criticism mandates a check for abnormality as well.

Criticisms being leveled at leisure research have been coming from many quarters. Aside from the possibility that there may be a group of abnormal critics of leisure research, those passing judgment on leisure research are apt to find some distinguished company. In fact, criticism of leisure research has been so common lately that one might even begin to characterize leisure research as a class of shortcomings. These shortcomings include, among others, excessive reliance on survey methodology, fascination with "number-crunching," allowing research method to dictate the research problem, and a gap between research writing and practitioner comprehension, (Bullock, 1983; Mannell, 1983; McLellan, 1980; Riddick, DeSchriver, & Weissinger, 1984; Stormann, 1983; Witt, 1983). In addition, the editor of the *Journal of Leisure Research* (Iso-Ahola, 1984) has admonished writers for the inappropriate marketing of statistics and mathematics in the journal.

The purpose here is not to reiterate or add to these criticisms. It is easy to take "potshots" at leisure research, especially when doing so appears to be so popular. Rather, I hope to contribute to what may be considered a reconstruction in leisure research. In order to accomplish this reconstruction it is necessary to address several key issues; including reconciliation of the rather arbitrary separation between objective data and subjective data, recognition of some other ways of knowing, and acknowledgement of research problems that cannot be answered adequately through traditional empirical methodologies alone.

NATURE OF DATA

Regardless of how we try to measure, prod, poke, operationalize, and objectivize "leisure experiencing" (a comprehensive term which includes the behavioral act and perceptions, beliefs, attitudes, and thoughts surrounding the act), it remains deceptive and subjective, defying conventional measurement. Witness the typical low percentages of explained variance which characterize leisure research. Perhaps such findings have prompted some (Mobily, 1984; Stormann, 1983) to protest the almost complete influence that empiricism exerts over leisure research. So much is made of the measurable, the antecedents and consequences of leisure behavior (Lewko & Crandall, 1980; Riddick et al., 1984), and so little of the subjective process of experiencing leisure. In short, "the man underneath" the behavior (Barrett, 1962, p. 276) has been ignored. Such an attitude has created a sentiment that the only acceptable knowledge is that attached to numbers (McLellan, 1980; Stormann, 1983). We have promoted a castelike epistemology, wherein certain "unscientific" ways of knowing are disparaged and labeled as opinion or idle speculation. The net result is a separation between behavior and emotionality, between objectivity and subjectivity. In our quest for certainty and the antecedent, or what the noted philosopher John Dewey referred to as the "unmoved mover," (1920, p. 20), or what empiricists might call "first causes," we have forgotten that we find only probabilities. In other words, we make the best bets (empirically) under the given circumstances and conditions relative to the leisure experiencing.

Despite continuing efforts to achieve it, objectivity in leisure research may be artificial. So-called objective measures remain part of the research subject's experiencing and are, therefore, subjective in spite of efforts to obtain "hard" data. Opinions, beliefs, and attitudes are no less subjective to the people experiencing them simply because numbers are used to represent those feelings. Even variables which we might think are reliably objective are often susceptible to criticism. Take, for instance, subjects' self-reported recreation participation based on recall. Initially one might say that such data are fairly objective. But as Dewey (1920, p. 104) put it, "time and memory are true artists; they remould reality nearer to the heart's desire." We often forget that perception is an active process for our subjects and that an event, phenomenon, or experience once perceived is actively altered, never quite the same as raw sense data.

Evidently, behavioral reports of leisure are not immune from such perceptual distortions. In a recent study of participation, Chase and Harada (1984) asked subjects to estimate the number of times they visited a swimming facility and then compared those estimates to the subjects' actual visits. The results indicated a substantial overestimation of visits by the subjects. While some errors in self-reports could be expected because of forgetting, the average overestimation (15.34 visits) found by Chase and Harada indicates that "sentiment" was truly at work among their subjects.

Findings such as these clearly bring the separation of objective and subjective in leisure research into question. As a large portion of research into leisure over the past few decades has emphasized self-reports and has taken those same reports as objective fact, much of the same could be reasonably classified as subjective because perception of leisure may well work its "halo effects" on what subjects thought they should have done, rather that what they actually did.

Thus, it may be a terrible mistake to follow the lead of physical science in social inquiry exclusively (cf. Dewey, 1939, pp. 949–950). Clearly, recall and perception and leisure are important qualitative and quantitative research problems, but researchers must begin to recognize that both methods have limitations. Although qualitative methodologists are frequently singled out as being "too subjective," the weaknesses of the empirical (quantitative) method have not passed unnoticed by other researchers in the social sciences. "A growing number of scholars in anthropology, economics, history, political science, and sociology are questioning just how scientific the social sciences can and should be" (Winkler, 1985, p. 5). Although the scientific method has dominated research in these fields since the Second World War, Winkler reported that dissatisfaction and disillusion with empiricism are increasing. Human behavior has not been very predictable, and humans do not tend to act very much like the biological entities to which the empirical method was first applied. This twofold recognition has prompted some investigators in the social sciences to call for a more interpretative and humanistic approach to the study of the social condition. Inasmuch as a great deal of the study of leisure qualifies as social inquiry, perhaps we should seek the counsel of our colleagues in the social sciences and humanities.

Objectivity and subjectivity may well reside on the same continuum when it comes to human experience. Nature and physical function do not advise separation, but rather a holistic perspective. For example, Selye's (1956) stress theory explicitly links the psychological and the physical in noting that many objective and verifiable physical maladies (e.g., ulcers) have their roots in the nonobjective affect. Likewise, even the objective machine is knowable as a machine only when its constituent parts are thought of as a whole, a collective, a unified thing (Dewey, 1929, p. 162). The point is that dualism is rarely witnessed in other phenomena. Feelings, words, ideas, and other qualitative, subjective measures are symbolic, just as numbers are symbolic. All symbols can be regarded as data. The fact that we have programmed computers to utilize one symbol system more efficiently than others does not justify the elevation of a numerical system of symbols at the expense of more subjective paradigms. All symbolic data are usuable.[2] We are challenged to bring other symbol systems up to the level of the numerical system.

Further, if leisure is thought of as a complex phenomenon, we can be assured that one symbol system will never do. One system will never bring us to the level of understanding and explanation we seek. Leisure is complex because it occurs in a historical context. Both James (1910/1963, p. 232) and Dewey (1939, p. 906) noted that complexity is a function of the potential an object has for combination and interaction with other objects. Leisure attains its complexity through context; it has a fundamental, basic quality which readily allows for combination with a variety of contextual substrates or objects. The result is observed as a complex phenomenon, which to our dismay frequently eludes objective measurement and escapes understanding when successfully reduced by objective measurement. Leisure is difficult to know apart from its combination with other experiential phenomena. Appropriately enough, leisure at its best is complex. It is no wonder that practitioners often fail to recognize the leisure talked about in a research report; it is too simple. Indeed, do we simplify leisure so much through research and measurement that it is no longer recognizable as leisure?

The importance of context might immediately suggest field study as an appropriate methodology. Yet we forget that the statistical control typical of field study is only another instance of the artificial. We substitute control by statistics for control by design. We neglect the careful observation characteristic of participant-observer studies as a necessary corollary to fieldwork. Qualitative research, used in conjunction with empirical methodologies, yields rich and complex data relative to leisure in context. Just as it is impossible to know a machine by studying a single gear, or to know a physiological system by studying one organ, so too it is impossible to know leisure in isolation. The real, sensible experience of leisure never exists apart from its stage—the rest of the real, sensible world. When we recall a leisure experience, we remember it along with its context, not as a pure form.

Evidence of the failure of researchers to recognize the complexity of leisure is apparent enough. For instance, Witt (1984) criticized the quality of literature reviews and the failure of researchers to place findings in the context of existing literature. Riddick et al. (1984) found that many studies do not check for the interactive effects of variables. Finally, Mannell (1983) noted that there are few uncomplicated routes to follow relative to research methods, questions, and definitions regarding leisure phenomena.

We do not think about leisure as a complex just as we fail to recognize leisure experience as a complex. We do not think of leisure as a symbol in combination with other symbols, but muse about it in simple, isolated terms. We are as guilty as the classical idealist for thinking in terms of pure "forms" instead of what Dewey calls the "compossibilities" (1929, p. 160) witnessed in leisure's interplay with other symbols. In sum, the tendency toward dualism and oversimplification in our research endeavors has resulted in a fuzzy picture of leisure at best—just the kind of portrait empiricism was meant to help us to avoid.

OTHER WAYS OF KNOWING

The complexity of leisure immediately suggests that we ought to attempt to know leisure in as many ways as possible. Unfortunately, it is obvious that there has been little agreement on what types of knowledge are most needed (Witt, 1984), aside from the unanimous support for empirically based knowledge. The calls for data-based research echo through our journals at regular intervals. But do we really advocate one method in preference to others, or are we just asking for more rigor? Confusing method with rigor may well explain the continued dissatisfaction with leisure research despite the wholesale adoption of the empirical method by the field.

Too often philosophy, history, or literature are associated with descriptors such as "subjective" or "conjecture." The speculative flavor of philosophy or the "dialogue with the past" (LaCapra cited in Winkler, 1985) characteristic of history are subjective in a sense, but still retain rigor. The sense of subjective that is being championed here is not the enthusiasm that Locke so distrusted or even akin to the notions of Transcendentialists like Coleridge or Parker. Rather, the sense of the subjective which qualifies as rigorous inquiry relies on nonnumerical data, observations made by philosophers, novelists, and social critics of the recent and distant past. Rigorous inquiry may also depend upon immersion of the researcher into the social context in order to make accurate observations, though such observations are qualitative in nature. Rigorous inquiry might even take an applied philosophy bent ("if, then" methodology), whereby a philosophical viewpoint is assumed to be true, and the researcher then attempts to deduce what logically follows with respect to a particular topic or human dilemma. In all of these subjective research ventures we see a sense of the subjective that can be equated with the rigor customarily reserved for empirical methods. It is not idle speculation or haphazard thinking or even undisciplined imagination at work here, but a careful, systematic, and reasoned approach.

Other methods of research are not so unlike hard data methodologies, if we use rigor as the criterion and not statistics. In fact, advocacy for qualitative methodologies, participant—observer research, case studies, and the like have found more frequent support lately (Bullock, 1983; Lewko & Crandall, 1980; Riddick et al., 1984). Regrettably, the emphasis on numerical knowing serves to continue a legacy of distrust of the arts (Dewey, 1929, p. 4) and the humanities as valid methods. Such an attitude serves to cast an aura of doubt around historical commentary, for example, even if it is written by well-respected historians. If we could think of historians, or philosophers, or novelists as expert observers, only reporting their findings in a different style than that to which we are accustomed, we would discover a rich and complex world of leisure contained within the writings. Take, for example, Dostoevsky's (1881/1957) chapter on The Grand Inquisitor in his famous work, *The Brothers Karamazov*. Few could read this chapter and not come away knowing more about freedom than before. Just as Dostoevsky teaches us how to talk about freedom, so too the novelist, philosopher, or historian can teach us how to talk about leisure. In fact, Dostoevsky's chapter is regarded as a classic discourse on freedom. Do we ignore it because it is fiction? I dare say Dostoevsky's rigor would be acceptable.

Besides employing other methods of knowing, researchers may increase the credibility of empirical methods by conducting a few subjective validation checks. Methods and findings should be checked for correspondence and coherence. Together, correspondence and coherence are manifest as thorough and relevant literature review sections and discussion sections (cited earlier as pressing problems in leisure research). Checking for coherence and correspondence will likely help investigators avoid the research report that is "without a beginning or an end" (Witt, 1984, p. 62)

Coherence and correspondence checks are easy enough. Though some might feel that such techniques are too ill defined, common sense was recognized by writers like James (1910/1963), Emerson (the "Universal Mind," 1841/1967) and existentialists like Barrett ("pre-conceptual wisdom," 1962, p. 213) as a legitimate precursor to more complex explanation and understanding. In fact, "what makes any proposition scientific is its power to yield understanding, insight, intellectual at-homeness, in connection with any existential state of affairs" (Dewey, 1939, p. 947).

Dewey's (1929/1939) method for checking correspondence and coherence is straightfoward and easily implemented. It entails assuming an idea, relationship, or even a research finding to be true and asking whether the supposition makes the world more luminous or clearer. In short, does it makes the world more coherent and understandable? Whether the effort is basic or applied, referring research results back to experience assures a sort of relevance often conspicuously absent from leisure research.

Likewise, reflective thought should be checked against experience. Symbols, in the form of ideas can be used to "act without acting" (Dewey, 1929, p. 151). Bearing in mind the inductive and probabilistic nature of a research venture, objective or otherwise, we seek to implement our result as an "end in view" (Dewey, 1929, p. 150) in order to discern a clearer picture of leisure experiencing. By considering the experiential possibilities of symbolic thought we may come to uncover probable causes.

Therefore, probable explanations under existing circumstances, which become part of a continuous dialectic process, are a function of both objective and subjective ways of knowing. Cooperative methods are needed where one method alone will not make leisure phenomena more coherent, understandable, and explainable.[3]

PROBLEMS WHICH DEFY EMPIRICISM

In the area of action and conduct toward one another, moral and ethical philosophy has exerted a greater influence than empiricism. As leisure is a value-laden concept, research into ethics and leisure seems entirely appropriate. But the area of ethics as a topic in leisure research has been of little concern, save some recent efforts by Fain (1984). Perhaps it is because questions of right and wrong are not important problems to address when researching leisure. But Hemingway (1985) has suggested a different explanation:

> The empirical claim and the value claim are fundamentally different, with the former derived from a logical positivist and empiricist tradition that denies meaning to values because they can neither be validated by experience or subsumed under general laws of nature based on recurrence of phenomena. (p. 45)

In short, the relationship between the research method and the research problem may be suspect at times. Most leisure researchers are schooled in the empirical method. This method dominates, and sometimes dictates, the research problem. The age-old difficulty of allowing method to precede and determine the problem has not often brought leisure researchers to the arena of ethics because the empirical method we know so well does not help much in answering questions of right and wrong (cf. Hemingway, 1985).

True, we could take a poll and have people rate leisure activities along a continuum of goodness and badness, but empirically gathered opinion does not tell us what *ought* to be understood as good or bad leisure. To a certain extent, the free-market system in this country allows each citizen an ethical vote with respect to good leisure choices. Few of us would be comfortable in saying that the leisure choices made by Americans are always the best ones. And what of freedom? Should people be self-determined in their leisure? Few of us would reply "No," but what is the practitioner to do when constituents make consistently bad choices—witness, for instance, substance abuse as a common, self-determined leisure form. When should the practitioner intervene, and when is such intervention justified against the ideal of allowing complete choice in leisure? Moral and ethical problems do not lend themselves to empirical solutions. Ironically enough, however, moral and ethical solutions may also be considered probabilities (Dewey, 1929, p. 278) or answers to questions of right and wrong which may *usually* be correct under specified circumstances.

From the preceding perspective, it is not so difficult to see that subjective and objective methods can complement one another. We do not find it difficult to believe that a subjective theory can and should be used as a basis for empirical investigation. (And is a theory anything more than someone's rigorously determined estimate regarding what is probably true?) But we rarely consider the opposite—that, in fact, some inquiry may only begin with empirical findings. Too often we stop with empirical results, satisfied to accept low levels of explained variance and discounting the remainder as extraneous variance. Instead of acquiescing, we need to use objective findings as "instumentalities" (Dewey, 1929, p. 284) to further enhance the probabilistic explanations we seek. Understanding is facilitated by allowing objective and subjective explanation to interact in order to suggest new possibilities to test. The net result of this reconstructed and symbiotic approach to leisure research would be a continuous dialectic, still with "ends in view" or probabilities, but probabilities which lead to improved ideas (Dewey, 1939, p. 856). It follows that improved ideas suggest new possibilities which are tested through further observation and so on—the continuous dialectic.

As a case in point, consider the role philosophy might assume in employing an empirical finding as an instrument to better realize understanding of some leisure phenomenon. In such a situation philosophy might well act as a liaison between science and experience or between science and achievable possibilities (Dewey, 1929, p. 311, p. 313). Similarly, rigorous philosophical thought could act as a go-between to accomplish a reconciliation of empirical findings about, for instance, perceived freedom and the ethical question of self-determination.

Other examples of collaboration among the various modes of knowing could be cited. The point to ponder is that only through cooperative inquiry can the understanding of leisure be enriched. In the end we strive to think better thoughts so that we may ask better questions. This is the value of a reconstructed approach to our inquiry into leisure.

CONCLUSIONS

Clearly the empiricist and philosopher, the scientist and historian strive for the same thing when it comes to leisure research. Regardless of method, we all want to understand leisure as best as we can. In our inquiries we share the goal of attaining the most probably or plausible explanation under known circumstances and within relevant contexts.

We are not as much at odds as we might initially think. The artificial barriers which have been erected alienate the quantitative and qualitative. Recognize that there are many avenues to rigorous inquiry. If methodologies remain estranged from one another, if dialogue does not begin, then we will all be guilty of trying to explain too little. We will, as Hemingway (1985) puts it, "impoverish ourselves and our profession" (p. 48). All are culpable in this regard. Complacency has led to alienation, and alienation has led to an aritifical dualism. And the separation is our greatest enemy.

I leave you with the following quote from William James (1907/1978) to reflect upon: "the greatest enemy of any one of our truths may be the rest of our truths" (p. 306).

So often truths have a tendency toward self-preservation and seek to extinguish whatever contradicts them (cf. Hemingway, 1985, p. 46).

REFERENCES

Barrett, W. (1962). *Irrational man*. Garden City, NY: Doubleday Anchor Books.
Bullock, C. C. (1983). Qualitative research in therapeutic recreation. *Therapeutic Recreation Journal, 17*, (4), 36–43.
Chase, D. R., & Harada, M. (1984). Response error in self-reported recreation participation. *Journal of Leisure Research, 16*(4), 322–329.
Dewey, J. (1939). *Intelligence in the modern world*. New York: Random House.
Dewey, J. (1920). *Reconstruction in philosophy*. New York: Holt.
Dewey, J. (1929). *The quest for certainty*. New York: Putnam.
Dostoevsky, F. (1957). *The brothers Karamozov*. New York: Signet (Original work published in 1881).
Emerson, R. W. (1967). The conservative. In M. Van Doren (Ed.), *The portable Emerson* (pp. 89–109). Canada: Viking. (Original work published 1841).
Fain, G. (1984). Toward a philosophy of moral judgment and ethical practices in leisure counseling. In T. Dowd (Ed.), *Leisure counseling* (pp. 277–300). Springfield, IL: Thomas.
Hemingway, J. L. (1985). Recreation, therapy, and society. In K. E. Mobily (Ed.),

Proceedings of the second annual therapeutic recreation research colloquium (pp. 40–49). Iowa City: The University of Iowa.
Iso-Ahola, S. E. (1984). Editor's notes: What is appropriate for publication? *Journal of Leisure Research, 16*(4), iv–v.
James, W. (1978). How is truth established? On pragmatic grounds. In J. A. Gould (Ed.), *Classic philosophical questions* (pp. 298–306). Westerville, OH: Merrill (Original work published 1907).
James, W. (1963) *Pragmatism and other essays*. New York: Pocket Books (Original work published 1910).
Lewko, J., & Crandall, R. (1980). Research trends in leisure and special populations. *Journal of Leisure Research, 12*(1), 69–79.
Mannell, R. C. (1983). Research methodology in therapeutic recreation. *Therapeutic Recreation Journal, 17*(4), 9–16.
McLellan, R. (1980). Research. *Parks and Recreation, 15*(7), 62–67, 90.
Mobily, K. E. (1984). The state of leisure research: Ten miles from nowhere. *Leisure Commentary and Practice, 3*(5), 1–3.
Riddick, C. C., DeSchriver, M., & Weissinger, E. (1984). A methodological review of research in Journal of Leisure Research from 1978 to 1982. *Journal of Leisure Research, 16*(4), 311–321.
Rosen, B. (1978). *Strategies of ethics*. Boston: Houghton Mifflin.
Selye, H. (1956). *The stress of life*. New York: McGraw-Hill.
Stormann, W. F. (1983). The costs of professional recognition. *Leisure Commentary and Practice, 2*(3), 1–3.
Winkler, K. J. (1985). Questioning the science in social science, scholars signal a 'turn to interpretation.' *The Chronicle of Higher Education, 30*(17), 5–6.
Witt, P. A. (1984). Research in transition. *Parks and Recreation, 19*(5), 60–63.
Witt, P. A. (1983). The ever present researcher-practitioner gap. *Leisure Commentary and Practice, 2*(1), 1–3.

NOTES

1. Title on loan from Dewey's (1920) *Reconstruction Philosophy*. An earlier version of this paper was presented at the 1985 Leisure Research Symposium, Dallas, TX.

2. One reviewer of this manuscript contended that the weakness may not be with the data, but with theories, meanings, and explanations offered for the data by leisure scholars. This is certainly an alternative perspective that should be pursued, but I still maintain my position. Furthermore, could it be that our theories are inadequate because we rely too much on only one way of thinking about leisure—the empirical way?

3. A short comment relative to theory building seems warranted, for certainly the paucity of theory in leisure research has attracted a fair share of criticism (Bullock, 1983; Mannell, 1983; Riddick, et al. 1984). Few of us spend enough time just thinking. If we do not reflect and consider the possibilities of leisure in an experiential world, we fail to project reasonable and probable theories. Indeed the function of reflective thought is two fold: the check for coherence and correspondence, and theorizing via the possibilities of symbols. In effect, theorizing may be "characterized by excursion from the actual into the possible" (Dewey, 1939, p. 854). Few musings are better suited to the inductive nature of leisure research than "playing" with symbols as possibilities.

2

APPLIED BEHAVIOR ANALYSIS: TECHNOLOGICAL OFFERINGS FOR THERAPEUTIC RECREATION

Jennifer J. Trap
John O. Cooper

Although thoroughly documented in the literature, applied behavior analysis is a methodological approach about which misconceptions frequently exist and which has had limited use in the domain of leisure behavior. This statement is particularly relevant to the practice of therapeutic recreation, an environment in which applied behavior analysis has much to offer. This article provides a basic analysis of the components of applied behavior analysis, relates its use to the increasing demands for accountability, and illustrates the application of applied behavior analysis within the context of single subject research.

The practice of applied behavior analysis is documented thoroughly in the literature. Cooper (1982) reported that approximately 25 journals, including the *Journal of Applied Behavior Analysis, The Behavior Analyst,* and *Education and Treatment of Children,* are devoted almost entirely to applied behavior analysis. In spite of this documentation and information, many professionals have misconceptions concerning what applied behavior analysis has to offer therapeutic recreation. This article will describe the dimensions of applied behavior analysis along with the contribution this technology and practice offers therapeutic recreation in the following areas: systematic applications, direct and frequent measures, and experimental methodology.

APPLIED BEHAVIOR ANALYSIS

The origins of applied behavior analysis are found in basic laboratory research known as the experimental analysis of behavior. The dimensions of this applied behavior were defined by Baer, Wolf, and Risley (1968). They stated "the study must be applied, behavioral, and analytic; in addition, it should be technological, conceptually systematic, and effective, and it should display some generality" (p. 92). The key terms within this quote were precisely defined by Baer et al. (1968). They will be briefly described in this article.

Applied was used to describe research involved with behaviors that are currently important to society as well as individuals. In this sense, *applied* was not necessarily defined by research procedures utilized in a particular study.

The focus of applied *behavioral* research is the manipulation of stimuli in the environment for the purpose of helping individuals emit specific behaviors that are important to the clients or society. The emphasis here is on the actions of individuals rather than their statements, unless their verbal behavior is under study. Reliable quantification through precise measurement is a critical aspect of applied behavior analysis.

Applied as well as nonapplied behavioral research is concerned with the control of behavior. Baer et al. (1968) noted that the analysis of behavior required believable demonstrations of events responsible for the occurrence or nonoccurrence of these specific behaviors. *Analytic*, then, refers essentially to the demonstration of this functional relationship between the behavior and interventions. Single-case experimental designs such as the multiple baseline, reversal, and the multielement have been commonly used to demonstrate analytic control of specific behaviors (Johnston & Penneypacker, 1980; Tawney & Gast, 1984).

Effective means that the demonstrated change in client behavior is large enough for practical value. In other words, practitioner-researchers should ask if the desired behavior change was socially important?

Technological is defined as a set of specific procedures for behavioral applications. The description of procedures should include enough detail for the naive reader to implement those procedures. It is not enough to say that the therapeutic recreation specialist used social reinforcement. For social reinforcement to be a technical description, each component (e.g., schedule, contingency, immediacy) would need to be specified along with the specific verbal statements that would be used ("Super performance! Your time shows great improvement," etc.).

There are two types of generalization (Sulzer-Azaroff & Mayer, 1978). Both types require durability over time (Stokes & Baer, 1977). Stimulus generalization occurs when the behavior change transfers to nontrained or nontherapeutic settings, or when the behavior transfers across clients. Response generalization occurs when one class of behavior transfers to other classes of behavior when the first class is modified, reinforced, punished, etc. For example, reinforcement of particular verbal statements may be accompanied by other verbal responses that are similiar but not identical to the reinforced verbal statements.

Applied researchers in some human service fields have undertaken research within the dimensions specified by Baer et al. (1968). For example in spite of the lack of a research base, the field of special education has shown tremendous growth as a field (Tawney & Gast, 1984). During the past 20 years, single-case experimental research has been used to identify critical classroom behaviors and document the effectiveness of strategies intended to change those behaviors.

Olsson (1986) noted that although the prospective payment system based on diagnostically related groupings (DRGs) initially exempted agencies such as psychiatric hospitals, rehabilitation centers, long-term care hospitals, and children's hospitals, those agencies are now targeted to be included under this system after their final review date in 1985. Olsson (1986) noted that there are several implications for therapeutic recreation specialists related to this development. The first implication identified was that therapeutic recreation specialists must become more scientific in all phases of their documentation to prove the contributions of their services to the client's rehabilitation and by reduction of the client's length of stay at such an agency. Application of single-subject research methodology would allow the therapeutic recreation specialist not only to document client performance but also to demonstrate a functional relationship between treatment strategies and actual client progress. Another implication was that therapeutic recreation managers should be concerned with increasing the productivity of their staff members. As Siedentop (1986) indicated, because of this opportunity to document efficiently and efffectively client progress as a function of the strategies and interventions employed, the practitioner may be reinforced. This reinforcement should assist in increasing productivity of staff. In some human services fields this technology has been applied directly to the performance of staff as well. Documented increases in staff performance have been demonstrated as a function of applied behavior analysis.

Applied researchers in therapeutic recreation employing the dimensions of applied behavior analysis as defined by Baer et al. (1986) could make at least three important contributions for therapeutic recreation specialists: (a) an initial research foundation for the systematic applied procedures used to decrease, increase, develop, or maintain leisure and leisure-related behaviors; (b) an emphasis on objective, frequent, and direct measurement; and (c) the development of single-case experimental methodology that would allow therapeutic recreation specialists to be practitioners of applied research.

SYSTEMATIC AND APPLIED PROCEDURES

Compton (1984), Mannell (1983), and Witt (1984) stated that there is a critical need to develop effective procedures to allow therapeutic recreation specialists to become more accountable in practice and research. Dattilo (1986) reported that single-subject research methodology allows the designing of applications that document a functional relationship between planned interventions and documented behavior change. The application of this methodology clearly shows one way to respond to Compton's (1984) research suggestions since evidence would be available that recreation, as a treatment strategy, can improve a client's leisure functioning.

Students enrolled in an introductory course of the study of principles of behavior often claim that the principles (e.g., reinforcement, punishment, extinction) are not new. They often report descriptions of how they have applied these principles without knowing the name of the procedures they have implemented.

Many report learning these principles through trial-and-error experiences or from experiences with highly skilled professionals. Therapeutic recreation specialists often encourage and reinforce leisure behaviors with praise. Public posting of performance (Van Houten, 1984) is one technique for improving performance behavior that could be easily implemented in many therapeutic recreation settings. Many therapeutic recreation specialists program for generalization of leisure skills by emphasizing common elements of the skills, by utilizing different trainers, and by reinforcing the behavior in other settings. Therapeutic recreation specialists may punish behaviors with verbal reprimands. They may try to reduce inappropriate behavior by reinforcing more positive behaviors (active participation) that are incompatible with the behaviors targeted for reduction. These therapeutic recreation specialists use the principles of behavior because in the past they have found these principles effective in improving many behaviors of special clients. Many times, however, therapeutic recreation specialists are unaware of their applications. They may feel uncomfortable with the terms "operant conditioning" or "behaviorism" whereas in practice they may have become masters in applying some principles of behavior through trial-and-error experiences.[1] Therefore, what can the science of applied behavior analysis offer therapeutic recreation specialists?

First, a foundation for the systematic utilization or application of environmental variables is now available. When a behaviorally oriented therapeutic recreation specialist uses reinforcement to maintain, increase, or develop target behaviors, considerations are given to specific variables. Target behaviors and consequences of behavior are clearly defined and applied (e.g., reinforcement is to produce specific client outcomes). In general, consequences employed by many therapeutic recreation specialists and other human service professionals may not be this systematic or consistent.

Second, the need for each generation of therapeutic recreation specialists to rediscover the principles of behavior through trial-and-error methods, verbal reports, and observation is reduced. Applied behavioral research sets the occasion for preservice specialists and leaders to acquire skills in applying the principles of behavior before they graduate. Also, this may reduce the opportunity for beginning therapeutic recreation specialists to practice other less precise strategies and techniques for behavior change, because decisions regarding the application of strategies and techniques are based on documented client performance.

Third, as stated previously, general knowledge of the principles of behavior may not be new to many therapeutic recreation professionals.[1] However, the discovery of new information and establishing the generality of that information demand experimental demonstration. For example, many experimental demonstrations in applied behavior analysis have documented the generality of socially significant behavior changes across clients (e.g., senior citizens, behaviorally disordered individuals, developmentally delayed individuals), across settings (e.g., clinics, hospitals, camps, schools, community centers), and across professionals (e.g., recreation leaders, day-care staff members, residential treatment staff members) (Cooper, Heron, & Heward, 1987).

DIRECT AND FREQUENT MEASUREMENT

Human service professionals, including therapeutic recreation specialists and activity therapists, are subject to passing fads in providing service as a result of basing changes in practice on historical accidents, untested theories, and the statements and practices of influential individuals. Applied behavioral analysts have specified clear and complete procedures for the direct measurement of behavior, including rapidly changing behavior. By using direct and frequent measurement of leisure and leisure-related behaviors, therapeutic recreation specialists and activity therapists may be in a position to defend themselves against passing fads and other pressures for implementing unproven and undocumented strategies.

Direct Measurement

Direct measurement is concerned with the measurement of specific target behaviors identified for change or development. For example, direct measurement must provide data on client responses as they occur before, during, and after treatment in the actual leisure settings. Client responses on norm- referenced intelligence, aptitude, or achievement tests would not be considered direct measurements. As indirect measures, they usually do not provide sufficient information for planning interventions for individual clients. Direct and frequent measurement of specific behaviors can document the behavior change and give an indication of the magnitude of that change. This information is especially important for day-to-day programming for clients in therapeutic recreation settings (Glancy, 1986).

Frequent Measurement

Frequent measurement is the repeated measurement of the client's behavior of concern. For example, if the behavior is active participation in an aerobic exercise class, the leader may record the client's actual participation during each 60-minute class. In a quilting course, the instructor or specialist may measure and record the number of stiches per inch during each class session. These measures of client performance are used to evaluate client progress and the appropriateness of individual treatment strategies.

With an emphasis on direct and frequent measurement, data can be graphed and analyzed for trends in performance. The use of frequent measurement will minimize the probability of using erroneous client data obtained on an atypical day. Measurement tactics utilized for frequent measurement without recourse to outside observers include direct measurement of permanent products and observational recording procedures, including event recording, latency recording, duration recording, whole and partial interval recording, and momentary time sampling. A complete discussion of these procedures is found in Cooper et al. (1987), Sulzer-Azaroff and Mayer (1978), and Tawney and Gast (1984).

EXPERIMENTAL METHODOLOGY

The majority of models for experimentation in therapeutic recreation are not appropriate for leaders and specialists in many leisure settings. These models usually involve between-group comparisons which are beyond the resources of many recreation therapists. For example, to test experimentally the effects of an intervention on isolate behavior of a client in a leisure setting, the experimenter must find several isolate clients to receive the intervention. Additional isolate clients may be required to serve as a control group. Obviously, even on residential programs, staff members may not have the time or resources to do this type of applied research.

Siedentop (1986) indicated that single-subject research tactics are not new. The experimental logic and design strategies for single-subject research have a long and honored history in the natural sciences (e.g., pharmacology). Siedentop (1986) identified the following reasons for his use of single-subject research methods:

1. Quality experimental research can be done on limited resources.
2. Single-subject research is experimental rather than descriptive, and it is through experimentation that sciences progress most quickly.
3. The analysis/decision system of single-subject research is biased toward robust variables.
4. The cost-benefit ratio between time invested in learning research skills and research outcomes is favorable in single subject research.
5. Single-subject research is much more likely to be replicated and eventually to develop strong external validity.
6. Single-subject methods encourage one to do experiments with clients in ways that the clients' behavior changes for the better.

These reasons for the use of single-subject research methods may be true for many therapeutic recreation specialists. Application and dissemination of single-subject research could begin the development of a much needed research base in therapeutic recreation.

Historically, therapeutic recreation has not demonstrated a cumulative development of applied practices (Dattilo, 1986). This development can occur when therapeutic recreation specialists experimentally analyze their interventions.

Applied behavior analysis is characterized by defining both dependent and independent variables and systematically manipulating those independent variables with single subjects or groups (Hersen & Barlow, 1976). Therefore, it provides therapeutic recreation specialists and other human service professionals with the methodology of a "true" experimental approach to the analysis of procedures and techniques. For this reason, the use of single-subject (or single-case) experimental methodology in applied settings has developed rapidly during the past 25 years (e.g., Wolf, Risley, & Mees, 1964; Pierce & Risley , 1974; McClannahan & Risley, 1975; Schleien, Wehman, & Kiernan, 1981; and Cooper 1987). Applied researchers faced many problems during the early 1960s in the development, demonstration, and dissemination of single-case experimental methodolgy.

First, the absence of procedures and data on interobserver agreement on the occurrence or nonoccurrence of the dependent variable led to problems in interpreting results. Second, some existing designs (e.g., reversal, multiple baseline across subjects, multiple baseline across behaviors) presented unique problems in applied settings. For example, many administrators objected to the return to baseline conditions of the reversal design; many professionals objected to the number of baseline sessions needed for some subjects (or behaviors) in the multiple baseline across subjects (behaviors). Third, most journals in psychology, education, activity therapy areas, and other human services fields were hesitant in publishing studies in single-subject applied research.

In 1968, two significant events in applied behavior analysis occurred. First was the publication of the *Journal of Applied Behavior Analysis (JABA). JABA* was the first major journal focusing on applied behavior analysis in America. This publication gave researchers an outlet for publishing findings of single-case experimental research. Barlow (1981) has stated that *JABA* subscriptions outnumber all but the largest journals and "that major advances first reported in *JABA* have affected every aspect of our functioning" (p. 1).

The second event that influenced applied research was again an outcome of the publication of *JABA*. Articles that appeared in *JABA* were used as model demonstrations of how to apply and interpret single-case experimental methodology. Over the years since the initial publication of *JABA*, studies reported have shown improvement in both application and experimental design. Three significant examples of these changes were the requirement and call for reporting interobserver agreement measures on the occurrence or nonoccurrence of the dependent variable, social validity measures, and establishing the intergrity of the independent variable.

The methodology of single-case analysis increased rapidly during the 1970s. Examples of the major developments included (a) the demonstration and explanation of three less common designs for applied settings; (b) the multielement baseline design (Ulman & Sulzer-Azaroff, 1975); (c) the changing criterion design (Hartman & Hall, 1976); and (d) the multiple probe baseline design (Horner & Baer, 1978). The call for improved procedures to check or verify interobserver agreement (Kazdin, 1977) and for social validity considerations (Wolf, 1978) led to improved studies. In 1976 the first major textbook devoted to single-case experimental designs in applied settings (Hersen & Barlow, 1976) was published. These methodological developments impacted on the conceptualization and dissemination of single-case experimental research.

As a result of the development of single-case experimental research during the last 25 years, therapeutic recreation personnel are now in a position to use analysis techniques in their agencies. Many therapeutic recreation specialists are uniquely positioned to perform analysis that can lead to significant advances in providing leisure services to special clients. With an increasing application of behavior analysis in therapeutic recreation, the field would begin to be able to incorporate a more precise and scientific approach into its practices.

REFERENCES

Baer, D. M., Wolf, M. M., & Risley, T.R. (1968). Some current dimensions of applied behavior analysis. *Journal of Applied Behavior Analysis, 1,* 91–97.

Barlow, D. H. (1981). Editorial. *Journal of Applied Behavior Analysis, 14,* 1–2.

Compton, D. M. (1984). Research priorities in recreation for special populations. *Therapeutic Recreation Journal, 1,* 9–17.

Cooper, J. O., Heron, T. E., & Heward, W. L. (1987). *Applied behavior analysis.* Westerville, OH: Charles E. Merrill.

Cooper, J. O. (1982). Applied behavior analysis in education. *Theory Into Practice, 21* (2), 114–118.

Cooper, J. O. (1981). *Measuring behavior.* Westerville, OH: Charles E. Merrill.

Dattilo, J. (1986). Single-subject research in therapeutic recreation: Applications to individuals with disabilities. *Therapeutic Recreation Journal, 20* (1), 6–87.

Dattilo, J. & Barnett, L. A. (1985). Therapeutic recreation for individuals with severe handicaps: An analysis of the relationship between choice and pleasure. *Therapeutic Recreation Journal, 19* (3), 79–91.

Glancy, M. (1986). Participant observation in the recreation setting, *Journal of Leisure Research, 18* (2), 59–80.

Hartmann, D. P., & Hall, R. V. (1976). The changing criterion design. *Journal of Applied Behavior Analysis, 9,* 527–532.

Hersen, M., & Barlow, D. H. (1976). *Single case experimental designs.* New York: Pergammon Press.

Horner, R. D., & Baer, D. M. (1978). Multiple-probe technique: A variation on the multiple baseline. *Journal of Applied Behavior Analysis, 11* 189–196.

Johnston, J. M., & Pennypacker, H. S. (1980). *Strategies and tactics for human behavioral research.* Hillsdale, N.J.: Lawrence Erlbaum Associates, Inc.

Journal of Applied Behavior Analysis. (1968-1985). Lawrence, KS: Society for the Experimental Analysis of Behavior.

Kazdin, A. E. (1977). Artifact, bias and complexity of assessment: The ABCs of reliability. *Journal of Applied Behavior Analysis,10,* 141–150.

Mannell, R. C. (1983). Research methodology in therapeutic recreation. *Therapeutic Recreation Journal, 17,* 9–16.

McClannahan, L. E., & Risley, T. R. (1975). Design of living Environments for nursing home residents: increasing participation in recreation activities. *Journal of Applied Behavior Analysis, 8,* 261–268.

Olsson, R. H. (1986). The prospective payment system: Implications for therapeutic recreation. *Therapeutic Recreation Journal, 20* (1), 7–17.

Pierce, C. H., & Risley, T. R. (1974). Improving job performance of neighborhood youth corps aides in an urban recreation program. *Journal of Applied Behavior Analysis, 7,* 207–215.

Schleien, S. J., Wehman, P., & Kiernan, J. (1981). Teaching leisure skills to severely handicapped adults: An age-appropriate darts game. *Journal of Applied Behavior Analysis, 14,* 513–519.

Siedentop, D. (1986). Why Single-subject research? in J.J. Trap, (Ed.), *Proceedings of the third therapeutic recreation research colloquium.* Columbus, OH: Phoenix Press.

Stokes, T. F., & Baer, D. M. (1977). An implicit technology of generalization. *Journal of Applied Behavior Analysis, 10,* 349–367.

Sulzer-Azaroff, B., & Mayer, G. R. (1977). *Applying behavior-analysis procedures with children and youth.* New York: Holt, Rinehart & Winston.

Tawney, J. W., & Gast, D. L. (1984). *Single subject research in special education.* Westerville, OH: Charles E. Merrill.

Ulman, J. D., & Sulzer-Azaroff, B. (1975). Multielement baseline design in educational research. In E. Ramp, & G. Semb (Eds.), *Behavior analysis: Areas of research and application.* Englewood Cliffs, NJ: Prentice-Hall.

Van Houten, R. (1984). Setting up performance feedback systems in the classroom. In W. L. Heward, T. E. Herson, D. S. Hill, & J. Trap-Porter (Eds.), *Focus on behavior analysis in education.* Westerville, OH: Charles E. Merrill.

Witt, P. (1984). Research in transition: Prospects and challenges. *Parks and Recreation, 19,* 60–63.

Wolf, M. M. (1978). Social validity: the case for subjective measurement on how applied behavior analysis is finding its heart. *Journal of Applied Behavior Analysis, 11,* 203–214.

Wolf, M. M., Risley, T. R., & Mees, H. (1964). Application of operant conditioning procedures to the behavior problems of an autistic child. *Behavior Research and Therapy, 1,* 305–312.

NOTE

1. Behaviorism refers to the philosophical and theoretical foundation of the

science of behavior analysis. Operant conditioning encompasses both punishment and reinforcement which are defined by their effect on behavior. Operant behavior is behavior which is controlled by its consequences (Cooper, Heron, & Heward, 1986).

3

CAUSAL PREDOMINANCE AMONG WORK, DYADIC, LEISURE, AND LIFE SATISFACTION ASSUMING A SPILLOVER MODEL

Richard S. Trafton
Howard E. A. Tinsley

Six models of the causal relationships among work, leisure, life, and dyadic (i.e., primarily but not exclusively marital; includes unmarried cohabitants) satisfaction were tested using data obtained from samples of blue-collar workers employed in a large city and a rural area of the midwest. The data were generally consistent with the spillover hypothesis of the relationship between work and leisure. The evidence supported the conclusion that work satisfaction is casually predominant to dyadic, leisure, and life satisfaction.

It has long been argued that marriage, work, and leisure play important parts in determining an individual's mental health and satisfaction with life (e.g., Cotgrove, 1965; Kornhauser, 1965; Tinsley & Tinsley, 1986). Three models have been posited to account for the observed relationships among work, leisure, and life satisfaction. The spillover of generalization model postulates that a worker's experiences on the job carry over into the nonwork aspects of his or her life so that a similarity develops in the pattern of work and nonwork life. Persons whose behavior conforms to the spillover model engage in work and nonwork activities which are similar in most aspects. The compensation model posits a negative association between work and nonwork. According to this hypothesis, the work situation is likely to be deficient in satisfying some needs of the worker. The worker compensated for these deficiencies by choosing leisure and family activities which will satisfy the needs not satisfied in the work situation. The segmentalist model hypothesizes that individuals segment or compartmentalize their life experiences so that experiences in one sphere of life (e.g., work) are regarded as separate and unrelated to experiences in other spheres of life (e.g., leisure). Following this line of reasoning, we would expect very little causal relationship between work and nonwork satisfaction.

A number of investigations have attempted to explicate the relationships between these areas of activity (marriage, work, and leisure) and satisfaction with life (Andrews & Crandall, 1976; Beard & Ragheb, 1980; Buchanan, 1983; Cooper & Robinson, 1987; London, Crandall, & Seals, 1977; Miller & Sjoberg, 1973; Ragheb & Griffith, 1982; Tinsley, Colbs, Teaff, & Kaufman, 1987; Trafton & Tinsley, 1980). London et al. (1977) and Trafton and Tinsley (1980), for example, noted the postive relationships predicted by the spillover model among job, dyadic, and leisure satisfaction. A review by Staines (1980) reported general support for the spillover hypothesis across a variety of data (e.g., level of involvement, skills, abilities, cultural pressures). A review by Kabanoff (1980), however, concluded that there was little support in the literature for either the spillover or compensation hypothesis. Tinsley (1984) found support for both models, but the compensation factor accounted for less of the variance in the psychological benefits of leisure than any other factor. Given the contradictory evidence bearing on this issue, a low priority should be assigned to further investigations of the relative merits of causal models which explain the relationships among the work and nonwork aspects of life and their impact on mental health and life satisfaction. Rather, a more thorough study of the merits of specific causal models appears to be necessary.

The purpose of this research is to explore six alternative hypotheses regarding the causal relationships among work, dyadic, leisure, and life satisfaction. The six hypotheses investigated in this research constitute every possible causal order among the three variables selected for study, assuming a spillover model.

Thus, the purpose of this research is not to investigate the relative merits of the spillover, compensation, and segmentalists models. Rather, the primary focus of this research concerns the relative influence of work, leisure, and dyadic satisfaction on each other and on life satisfaction.

METHOD

Casual Models

Six hypotheses regarding the causal relationships among work, leisure, dyadic, and life satisfaction were investigated. In each hypothesis the primary interest focused on the extent to which life satisfaction was causally influenced by (i.e., could be predicted from a knowledge of) work, dyadic, and leisure satisfaction. The six hypotheses represented every possible ordering of the work, leisure, and dyadic satisfaction variables, thus allowing a test of the efficacy of every possible variant of the basic spillover model.

The six hypotheses can be separated into three groups based on which variable is posited as causally predominant (i.e., the variable which causally influences all the other variables under investigation). Models 1 and 2 hypothesize that work satisfaction exerts a causal influence on leisure, dyadic, and life satisfaction (see Table 1). Model 1 further hypothesizes that dyadic satisfaction has a causal influence on leisure and life satisfaction, but leisure satisfaction causally influences only life satisfaction (see Table 1). In contrast, Model 2 reverses the order of the two middle variables. In Model 2, leisure satisfaction is hypothesized to exert a causal influence on dyadic and life satisfaction (see Table 1), whereas dyadic satisfaction causally influences only life satisfaction. Thus, Models 1 and 2 might be labeled "work" models in that work satisfaction is hypothesized to influence nonwork satisfaction.

In contrast, Models 3 and 4 represent nonwork models in which the nonwork sources of satisfaction are hypothesized to influence work satisfaction. Model 3 hypothesizes leisure satisfaction as a cause of dyadic, work, and life satisfaction; Model 4 hypothesizes dyadic satisfaction as a cause of leisure, work, and life satisfaction (see Table 1). Finally, Models 5 and 6 represent "mixed models" in which work satisfaction is both caused by and a cause of some forms of nonwork satisfaction. In Model 5, dyadic satisfaction is hypothesized to cause work, leisure, and life satisfaction. Work satisfaction, in turn, causes leisure and life satisfaction, and leisure satisfaction exerts a causal influence only on life satisfaction (see Table 1). In Model 6, leisure satisfaction is hypothesized to be the primary causal variable, influencing work, dyadic, and life satisfaction. Work satisfaction is hypothesized to have a causal influence on dyadic and life satisfaction, whereas dyadic satisfaction is posited to have a causal influence on only life satisfaction (see Table 1).

Subjects

Two groups of subjects participated in the present study. Sample One consisted of 48 rank-and-file members of an industrial union in a densely populated midwestern metropolitan area. The average age of these subjects was 32.7 and approximately 80 percent were male. The instruments were administered in a group while the workers were attending a union education program at a local university. Anonymity was guaranteed and feedback was provided to the participants. Sample Two consisted of 67 first-line workers employed in a midwestern plant of a large manufacturer. Workers were recruited by posting a notice on plant bulletin boards. The notice indicated that all volunteers for the study would receive a "lottery ticket" for their participation. Winners of the lottery would receive small gifts (e.g., picnic cooler). The average age of these subjects was 34.3 and approximately 50 percent were male. These workers resided in a rural, economically depressed area. The average income of this group was approximately $5,000 per year less than that of Sample One. The data from Sample Two were collected in a group 1 hour before the start of the workers' shift. The combined sample represents a purposive sample rather than a random sample. Although probability statements cannot be made regarding the representativeness of the sample, the initial objective which guided the development of the purposive sampling plan was to obtain an arregate sample which represents a significant portion of the labor force.

Instruments

Trafton and Tinsley (1980) have investigated the internal

consistency reliability and the convergent and discriminant validity of the four instruments used in this study. Based on results obtained from a sample of 115 blue-collar workers, they concluded that the instruments demonstrated acceptable reliability and validity.

The 15-item Life Satisfaction Questionnaire (LSQ) was constructed by Trafton and Tinsley in a previous investigation to meet the need for a brief, reliable measure of life satisfaction. Forty-four Likert items relevant to life satisfaction, obtained from a number of sources (e.g., related instruments, interviews), were administered to 70 college students. Following an item analysis, the LSQ was reduced to the 15-item form used in this investigation. The LSQ items use the Likert format with seven response alternatives, ranging from completely agree to completely disagree (e.g., In general, I feel pessimistic about the future). Trafton and Tinsley (1980) report internal consistency reliabilities of .78 and .80 on samples of 70 college students and 115 blue-collar workers, respectively. The LSQ is scored by summing the individual's responses across the 15 items.

The 72-item Job Description Index (JDI; Smith, Kendall, & Hulin, 1969) was selected to measure job satisfaction. The directions instruct respondents to indicate whether each item describes their job by answering yes, no, or uncertain (e.g., My work is fascinating; My superior is annoying). The JDI yields a total job satisfaction score and satisfaction scores for five aspects of the job (i.e., work, supervision, co-workers, pay, promotion), each of which has been demonstrated to have good convergent and discriminant validity and to correlate with objective measures of satisfaction. Trafton and Tinsley (1980) reported an internal consistency reliability of .92 for the JDI total satisfaction score which was used in this research.

The 10-item Dyadic Satisfaction Scale (DSS; Spanier, 1976), based on the Marital Adjustment Scale (Locke & Wallace, 1959), was used to assess dyadic satisfaction (i.e., the satisfaction of married and unmarried cohabitants living in a dyadic relationship). The DSS instructs respondents to indicate the approximate extent of agreement between the respondents and their partners using a 6-point Likert scale with response alternatives ranging from all the time to never (e.g., How often do you confide in your partner?). Internal consistency reliabilities of .94 (Spanier, 1976) and .83 (Trafton & Tinsley, 1980) have been reported for the DSS, and a multitrait-multimethod investigation of the DSS revealed an acceptable level of construct validity (Trafton & Tinsley, 1980). Scores on the DSS are obtained by summing the individual's responses to the 10 items on the scale.

Overs, Tayler, and Adkins (1974) developed the Milwaukee Avocational Satisfaction Questionnaire (MASQ) to assess satisfaction with participation in leisure activities. The directions instruct respondents to answer each item in terms of how descriptive it is of their favorite leisure activity using a 5-point Likert scale with response alternatives ranging from "not satisfied" to "extremely satisfied" (e.g., The feeling of accomplishment I get from the activity). An internal consistency reliability of .89 was reported by Trafton and Tinsley (1980) for the MASQ. Trafton and Tinsley (1980) also reported an acceptable level of construct validity for the MASQ, based upon a multitrait-multimethod investigation of the instrument. Nevertheless, the evidence for the construct validity of the MASQ was weaker than the evidence supporting the validity of the other three instruments. Total scores on the MASQ are obtained by summing the responses to the 22 items on the scale.

Analysis

In order to obtain an estimate of the causal relationships among the variables, independent of the reliability of the instruments used, the correlations among the tests were adjusted for attenuation. The plausibility of the six hypothesized models was then evaluated using path analysis (Kenny, 1979; Nie, Hull, Jenkins, Steinbrenner, & Bent, 1975). It should be emphasized that path analysis cannot confirm or disconfirm a particular causal model. Rather, the technique requires the investigator to assume that (1) there is at least a weak causal order among the variables (i.e., the variables do not simply covary, but are causally related) and (2) the model is causally closed (i.e., variables outside the system are not responsible for the correlations among the variables in the model). Path analysis allows the investigator to determine the extent to which the hypothesized models accurately portray the correlations among the variables in the context of these two assumptions.

RESULTS

Table 1 presents the results of the six path analyses. For each model, the total covariance between each pair of variables is indicated as is the decomposition of the covariance into direct causal covariance, indirect causal covariance, and noncausal (i.e., spurious) covariance. Nie et al. (1975) describe the procedures used in the calculation of these covariances. Direct causal covariance represents the extent to which changes in the causally predominant (i.e., the independent) variable, effect concomitant changes in the causally subordinate (i.e., dependent) variable, without mediating influences from other sources. For example, an increase in job satisfaction directly produces an increase in life satisfaction. Indirect causal covariation represents the extent to which changes in the causally subordinate (i.e., dependent) variable are produced by the influence of the causally predominant (i.e., independent) variable on one or more intervening variables. For example, an increase in job satisfaction indirectly produces an inrease in life satisfaction by directly producing an increase in leisure satisfaction, which then directly produces the increase in life satisfaction. Any covariation remaining after direct and indirect effects are removed is attributed to spurious effects which can include, but are not limited to, sampling error, situational effects, and the influence of a common method of measurement.

As indicated in Table 1, the total causal covariance between leisure satisfaction and work, dyadic, and life satisfaction was significantly greater than zero in only 2 of 18 cases. In both instances (see Models 3 and 6), leisure satisfaction was observed to exert a significant causal influence on life satisfaction. In contrast, the total causal covariance significantly exceeded zero in 9 of the 18 analyses involving work satisfaction and 9 of the 18 analyses involving dyadic satisfaction. Because the MASQ has been shown to have lower levels of reliability and validity than the other measures used in this investigation (Trafton & Tinsley, 1980), and a significant relationship between leisure and life satisfaction was observed for two of the six hypothesized models, a conservative approach was adopted in interpreting this result. Instead of dropping leisure satisfaction from the model entirely, this finding was interpreted as an indication that any model in which leisure satisfaction was causally predominant to work or dyadic satis-

TABLE 1
Decomposition of Total Covariance among Pairs of Variables into Causal and Noncausal Covariance for Six Models of the Causal Relationships

Relationship	Total covariance	Causal covariance: Direct	Causal covariance: Indirect	Causal covariance: Total	Noncausal (spurious) covariance
Work predominant					
Model 1					
Work–dyadic	.24	.24	—	.24	—
Work–leisure	.15	.12	.03	.15*	—
Work–life	.53	.45	.08	.53	—
Dyadic–leisure	.17	.15	—	.15*	.02
Dyadic–life	.39	.26	.02	.28	.11
Leisure–life	.25	.13	—	.13*	.12
Model 2					
Work–leisure	.15	.15	—	.15*	—
Work–dyadic	.24	.22	.02	.24	—
Work–life	.53	.45	.08	.53	—
Leisure–dyadic	.17	.14	—	.14*	.03
Leisure–life	.25	.13	.04	.17*	.08
Dyadic–life	.39	.26	—	.26	.13
Nonwork predominant					
Model 3					
Leisure–dyadic	.17	.17	—	.17*	—
Leisure–work	.15	.12	.03	.15*	—
Leisure–life	.25	.13	.12	.25	—
Dyadic–work	.24	.22	—	.22	.02
Dyadic–life	.39	.26	.06	.20	.19
Work–life	.53	.45	—	.45	.08
Model 4					
Dyadic–leisure	.17	.17	—	.17*	—
Dyadic–work	.24	.22	.02	.24	—
Dyadic–life	.39	.26	.12	.39	—
Leisure–work	.15	.12	—	.12*	.03
Leisure–life	.25	.13	.05	.18*	.07
Work–life	.53	.45	—	.45	.08

continued

Relationship	Total covariance	Causal covariance Direct	Causal covariance Indirect	Causal covariance Total	Noncausal (spurious) covariance
Mixed predominance					
Model 5					
Dyadic–work	.24	.24	—	.24	—
Dyadic–leisure	.17	.15	.02	.17*	—
Dyadic–life	.39	.26	.13	.39	—
Work–leisure	.15	.12	—	.12*	.03
Work–life	.53	.45	.02	.47	.06
Leisure–life	.25	.13	—	.13*	.12
Model 6					
Leisure–work	.15	.15	—	.15*	—
Leisure–dyadic	.17	.14	.03	.17*	—
Leisure–life	.25	.13	.12	.25	—
Work–dyadic	.24	.22	—	.22	.02
Work–life	.53	.45	.06	.51	.02
Dyadic–life	.39	.26	—	.26	.13

*Not significantly greater than zero at .05 level of confidence.

faction (i.e., Models 2, 3, 4, and 6) was untenable.

Model 1 appeared to offer a slightly more plausible explanation of the causal relationships among the variables than Model 5. Model 1 (see Figure 1) orders the variables in order of the magnitude of their direct causal covariance, given the total causal covariance attributed to each source of satisfaction. This creates a more parsimonious model in which the need to explain relationships in terms of indirect causal covariance is minimized.

Reference to the results for Model 1 (Table 1) will help clarify the interpretation of Figure 1. The total covariance between work and life satisfaction is .53. The direct causal covariance (.45) is indicated in parenthesis. The indirect causal covariance (.08) is the sum of all the indirect causal influences, i.e., $[(.24 \times .26) + (.12 \times .13) + (.24 \times .15 \times .13)]$.

Path analysis also allows estimation of the influence of latent factors (E_1, E_2, and E_3 in Figure 1), or variables not specifically included in the model. The square of the path coefficients for these latent variables represents the proportion of variance in the

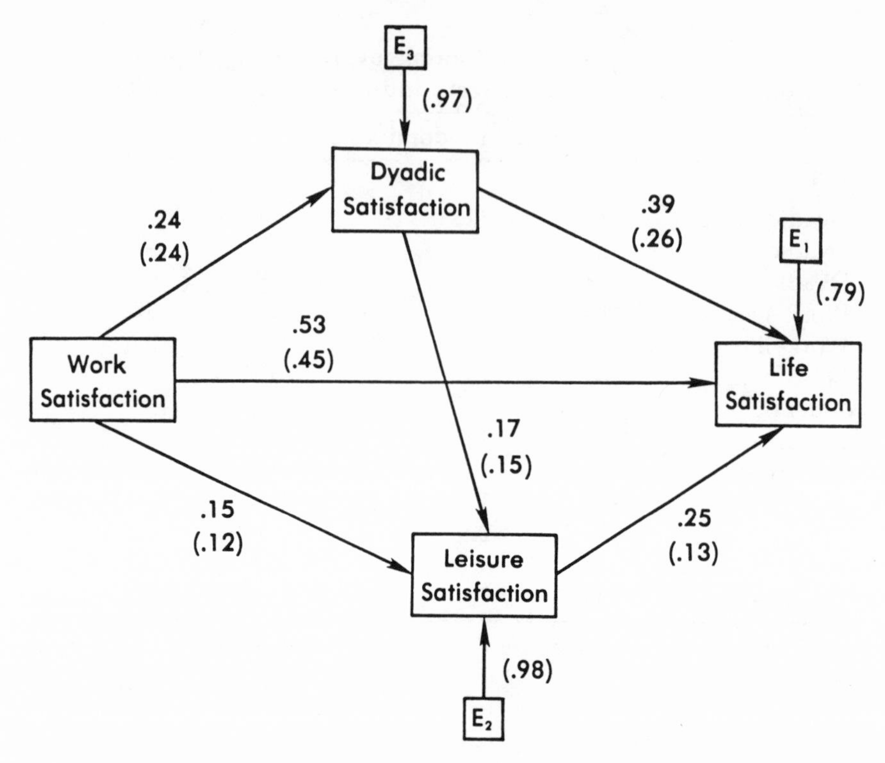

FIG. 1. Model of causal influences on life satisfaction illustrating the most parsimonious interpretation of the paths of causal influence.

particular variable not accounted for by all of the causally prior variables in the model. Figure 1 reveals that Model 1 accounts for 38 percent of the variance in life satisfaction, 4 percent of the variance in leisure satisfaction, and 6 percent of the variance in dyadic satisfaction.

DISCUSSION

The plausibility of six alternative models of the causal relationships among work, leisure, dyadic, and life satisfaction was investigated. The strongest support was obtained for Model 1 in which work satisfaction was postulated to exert both a direct causal influence on life satisfaction and an indirect causal influence on life satisfaction, which was mediated through the direct causal effects of work satisfaction on dyadic and leisure satisfaction.

Dyadic satisfaction is represented in Model 1 as having both a direct causal influence on life satisfaction and an indirect causal influence, which is mediated through its direct causal effect on leisure satisfaction. Although the direct causal effect of leisure satisfaction on life satisfaction was not significant in Model 1, Models 3 and 6 provided some evidence for such a causal relationship. Consequently, a conservative approach was adopted, and leisure satisfaction was retained in the final model. This investigation presents the first evidence of which we are aware bearing on the question of causal predominance among these variables.

The proportion of variance accounted for in life satisfaction (38 percent) is comparable to results obtained in similar studies (e.g., Sears, 1977). Moreover, the results are consistent with other work in this area (Kornhauser, 1965; London et al., 1977; Andrews & Crandall, 1976). Nevertheless, a large proportion of the variance in life satisfaction was unexplained. Although this may be due in large part to the fact that it was not our intention to explain life satisfaction, two other possibilities should be noted. First, even though the measures used in this study have demonstrated at least minimal levels of reliability and validity (Trafton & Tinsley, 1980), the tests may not be adequate measures of the variables under investigation. In this regard, the MASQ is the most questionable instrument used in this research. Our doubts about the MASQ led us to retain leisure satisfaction in the final model, despite its lack of significance in this investigation. Other investigations (e.g., London et al., 1977), for example, have found leisure satisfaction to contribute significantly to the individual's level of life satisfaction. We recommend the use of multiple measures of leisure satisfaction in future research on this issue until thoroughly validated measures of leisure satisfaction are available.

Second, it may be that a spillover model is not the best possible model for explaining the causal relationships among work, leisure and life satisfaction. Previous research (Staines, 1980) supports the conclusion that a spillover model is superior to the compensation model in explaining relationships among work and leisure satisfaction, but their applicability to an expanded model which includes dyadic and life satisfaction requires investigation. Furthermore, the validity of the segmentalist model (Kabanoff, 1980) remains largely uninvestigated.

Like many studies, this investigation raises more issues than it resolves. Because the findings from this investigation are consistent with those of London et al. (1977) and Sears (1977), they appear to have some generalizability. As such, they support the interpretation that the spillover hypothesis offers a plausible model of the relationships among work, leisure, dyadic, and life satisfaction, a finding consistent with the conclusion of Staines (1980). Going beyond this, however, the results reported herein suggest the possibility that work satisfaction is causally predominant to nonwork satisfaction. Questions about the psychometric properties of the MASQ must be addressed before this conclusion can be endorsed without reservation. Finally, this investigation leaves unanswered questions regarding the merits of the segmentalist hypothesis. Further research in this area is needed.

REFERENCES

Andrews, F. M., & Crandall, R. (1976). The validity of measures of self-reported well-being. *Social Indicators Research, 3*, 1–19.

Beard, J., & Ragheb, M. G. (1980). Measuring leisure satisfaction. *Journal of Leisure Research, 12*, 20–33.

Buchanan, T. (1983). Toward an understanding of variability in satisfactions within activities. *Journal of Leisure Research, 15*, 39–51.

Cooper, S. E., & Robinson, D. A. G. (1987). A comparison of career, home and leisure values of male and female students in engineering and the sciences. *Journal of College Student Personnel, 28*, 66–70.

Cotgrove, S. (1965). The relations between work and nonwork among technicians. *The Sociological Review, New Series, 13*, 121–129.

Kabanoff, B. (1980). Work and nonwork: A review of models, methods and findings. *Psychological Bulletin, 88*, 60–77.

Kenny, D. A. (1979). *Correlation and causality*. New York: Wiley Interscience.

Kornhauser, A. (1965). *Mental health of the industrial worker: A Detroit study*. New York: John Wiley & Sons.

Locke, H., & Wallace, K. (1959). Short marital adjustment and prediction tests: Their reliability and validity. *Marriage and Family Living, 21*, 251–255.

London M., Crandall, R., & Seals, G. (1977). The contribution of job and leisure satisfaction to quality of life. *Journal of Applied Psychology, 62*, 328–334.

Miller, P., & Sjoberg, G. (1973). Urban middle class life styles in transition. *Journal of Applied Behavioral Science, 9*, 144–162.

Nie, N. H., Hull, C. H., Jenkins, J. G., Steinbrenner, K., & Bent, D. H. (1975). *Statistical package for the social sciences*, 2nd Ed. New York: McGraw-Hill.

Overs, R. P., Taylor, S., & Adkins, C. (1974). *Avocational counseling in Milwaukee.* Final report on project H233466, Number 5D, Curative Workshop of Milwaukee, May.

Ragheb, M. G., & Griffith, C. A. (1982). The contribution of leisure participation and leisure satisfaction to life satisfaction of older persons. *Journal of Leisure*

Research, 14, 295–306.

Sears, R. R. (1977). Sources of life satisfaction of the Terman gifted men. *American Psychologist, 32,* 119–128.

Smith, P. C., Kendall, L. M., & Hulin, C. L. (1969). *The measurement of satisfaction in work and retirement: A strategy for the study of attitudes.* Chicago: Rand McNally & Co.

Spanier, G. (1976). Measuring dyadic adjustment: New scales for assessing the quality of marriage and similar dyads. *Journal of Marriage and the Family, 39,* 15–28.

Staines, G. L., (1980). Spillover versus compensation: A review of the literature on the relationship between work and nonwork. *Human Relations, 33,* 111–129.

Tinsley, H. E. A. (1984). The psychological benefits of leisure counseling (i.e., participation). *Society and Leisure 7,* 125–140.

Tinsley, H. E. A., Colbs, S. L., Teaff, J. D., & Kaufman, N. (1987). The relationship of age, gender, health, and economic status to the psychological benefits older persons report from participation in leisure activities. *Leisure Sciences, 9,* 53–65.

Tinsley, H. E. A., & Tinsley, D. J. (1986). A theory of the attributes, benefits, and causes of leisure experiences. *Leisure Sciences, 8,* 1–45.

Trafton, R. S., & Tinsley, H. E. A. (1980). An investigation of the construct validity of measures of job, leisure, dyadic and general life satisfaction. *Journal of Leisure Research, 12,* 34–44.

4

AN AUTOMATED MODEL FOR LEISURE ASSESSMENT: A WAY FOR COMMUNITY RECREATION PROGRAMS TO ADDRESS INDIVIDUAL NEEDS

Roy H. Olsson
Kathleen J. Halberg

Futurists suggest that organizations which provide services to the public will survive on a long-term basis only if they learn to address individual needs. This includes leisure service providers who have tended to provide leisure services on a mass basis with major concern to deliver those services in an efficient and effective manner. An essential and initial step to providing leisure services to meet individual needs is leisure assessment, which examines more than current desired leisure preferences.

An in-depth leisure assessment, the Leisure Diagnostic Battery, has been adapted for use with a microcomputer. The use of a microcomputer should make individual leisure assessment practical and feasible in terms of cost and time. The information obtained will provide a basis for the leisure service provider to begin to address individual needs.

The TLASCR (TRENDS Leisure Assessment Systems for Community Recreation) contains the following leisure assessments: Perceptions of Freedom in Leisure (Short Form); Perceptions of Freedom in Leisure (Original Version), which includes Perceived Leisure Competence, Perceived Leisure Control, Leisure Needs, Depth of Leisure Involvement, and Playfulness; Barriers to Leisure Involvement; Knowledge of Leisure Opportunities; and Leisure Preferences.

The long-term survivability of organizations dealing with the public at all levels will be determined by their ability to learn about and cater to their client's individual needs (Peters & Waterman, 1982). Gray and Greben (1974) came to a similar conclusion concerning recreation and park services. In their analysis of the status and future of the recreation and park movement, they suggested:

1. The U.S. has undergone massive social changes and reform that have produced significant, enduring consequences, among which a profound concern with the human values of all services to society, including recreation, has surfaced as the most prominent.
2. Park and recreation services as a whole have not addressed these changes but rather have clung to the status quo of providing programs based on material efficiency rather than concerns for individual human benefits.
3. If the recreation and park movement is to survive into the twenty-first century, it must begin to redefine its mission to include concerns for individual psychological well-being and needs.
4. To manifest this change, the recreation and park programs must become visionary in their future perspectives, mapping out a blueprint for meeting individual needs.

A key issue, before individual needs can be addressed, is first to determine what those individual needs are. Most current methods of needs assessment focus primarily on an individual's current, desired, and future activity preferences (Witt & Groom pp. 19–20). These assessments assume that leisure, and thus individual needs, can best be determined by the leisure activity in which the individual participates or desires to participate and fail to attempt to dicover why an individual participates in that activity (Iso-Ahola, 1980). Many current leisure theorists (Neulinger, 1981; Iso-Ahola, 1980; Murphy, 1981), suggest that additional variables, especially perceived freedom, are essential to experiencing leisure. Needs assessments, then, must also address issues beyond activity preferences if the meeting of individual needs is to be attempted.

Currently only one leisure assessment measures perceived freedom in leisure. That instrument is the Leisure Diagnostic Battery (LDB; Witt & Ellis,1984, 1987). The LDB also includes the ability to assess leisure preferences, barriers to leisure involvement, and knowledge of leisure oportunities.

THE LEISURE DIAGNOSTIC BATTERY

The LDB consists of 207 questions divided into eight scales. Five scales (A–E) combine to measure perceptions of freedom in leisure: (A) Perceived Leisure Competence (20 questions), which measures individual perceptions of the degree of cognitive, social, physical, and general competence in leisure experiences; (B) Perceived Leisure Control (17 questions), which measures individual perception of degree of internal control over leisure experiences; (C) Leisure Needs (20 questions), which measures individual ability to satisfy intrinsic needs such as relaxation, surplus energy, compensation, catharsis, optimal arousal, status, creative expression, skill development, and self-image via leisure experiences; (D) Depth of Involvement in Leisure Experiences (18 questions), which measures the extent to which the individual "flows" as it relates to Csikszentmihalyi's (1975) "flow" concept; and (E) Playfulness (20 questions), which measures the individual degree of playfulness based on Lieberman's (1977) play concepts, including cognitive spontaneity, physical spontaneity, social spontaneity, manifested joy, and sense of humor (Ellis & Witt, 1984, 1987).

Two scales (F and H) measure variables which potentially inhibit leisure participation: (F) Barriers to Leisure Involvement (24 questions), which identifies problems such as communication, social skills, decision making, desire/interest, time, lack of opportunity, lack of ability, financial, mental and accessibility the participant perceives while selecting and/or participating in leisure activities; and (H) Knowledge of Leisure Opportunities (28 questions), which measures individual knowledge of specific information, such as who can participate, what activities are available, where opportunities are present, when opportunities occur, and how much cost is involved in various activities as they relate to leisure (Ellis & Witt, 1987).

The final scale (G) Leisure Preference (60 questions) is used in the recreation and remediation programming process. It will measure the individual's preferred leisure activities, such as sports, arts and crafts, mental and linguistic activities, nature, music, and drama, as well as preferred style of participation, including active vs. passive, group vs. individual, and risk vs. nonrisk (Ellis & Witt, 1987).

In addition to the 95-question Perceived Freedom scale (A–E) described above, Witt and Ellis (1985) designed a short form assessment based on the 25 most reliable questions found within that 95-question scale. Although this method proved as reliable as the 95-question version at measuring perceived freedom, it does not allow for the assessment of perceived freedom in the five individual scale areas (perceived leisure competence, perceived leisure control, leisure needs, depth of involvement in leisure experiences, and playfulness), which is possible in the 95-question version. As a result, whereas the Perceived Freedom Short Form works well as a screening instrument, the long form would be needed if the score indicated a deficiency.

EFFICIENCY IN LEISURE ASSESSMENT

As the decade of the 1980s unfolded, the stark reality of Reaganomics and the new federalism became evident. Recreation and park programs, like other human services, took a back seat to national defense and reducing the national deficit (Gray & Greben, 1982). The impact on community recreation programs became clear; they would have to function with reduced staff and reduced budgets. Individual assessments as described above for most community recreation programs would not be feasible in terms of time and staffing. If future perspectives for meeting individual needs based on individualized leisure assessments were to become a reality, alternate solutions would have to be designed. Any proposed solution would have to address within its design independent usage by participants, that is to say, "Can participants take and score their own leisure assessment by themselves?"

One proposed solution designed by the Department of Leisure Studies and Services at the University of Oregon was to computerize the LDB. The final version for general recreation known as the TRENDS Leisure Assessment System for Community Recreation (TLASCR) was written on an Apple II computer and includes all scales from the LDB, the Perceived Freedom Short Form, and a personal data section (i.e., name, address, age, etc.).

A COMPUTERIZED MODEL FOR LEISURE ASSESSMENT

The assessment system described here has been written on

the Apple II system. It will work on the Apple II, II+, IIe, and IIc. In the future the TLASCR program should also be available on the IBM PC. The TLASCR is menu driven and has two components:

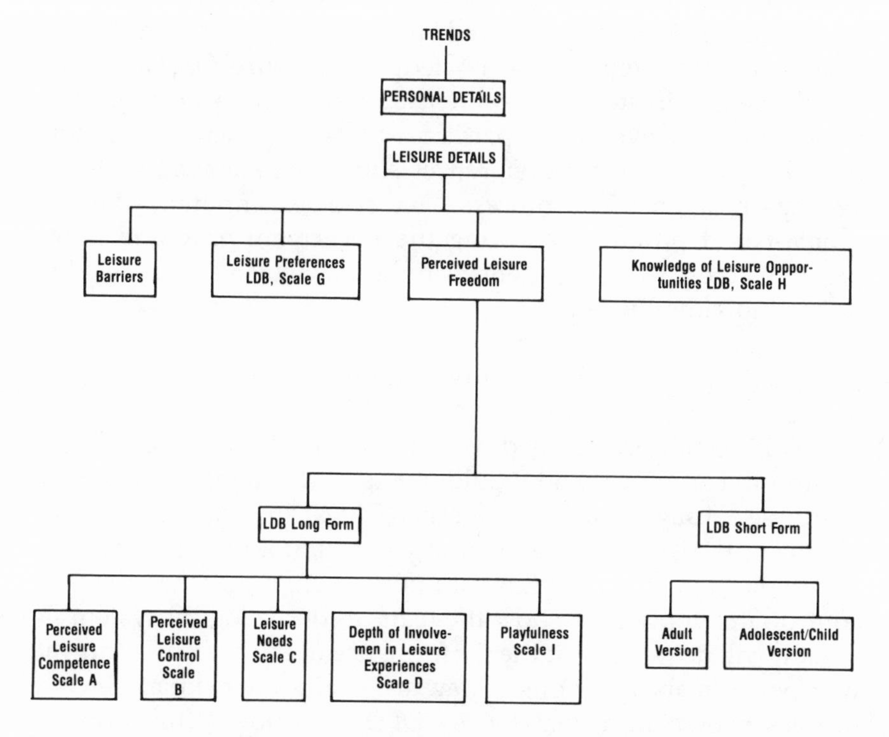

FIG. 1. Trends assessment options.

1. Personal Details will provide the recreator with demographic and social background information (i.e., age, sex, marital staus) and other information which is essential to becoming familiar with the participant and providing a basis for his or her programs.
2. The Leisure Details section, which is the area most central to the concerns of the recreator, was designed to allow a variety of options, each independently chosen. It includes the potential for leisure assessment in four areas:

1. Perceived Leisure Freedom
2. Leisure Barriers
3. Leisure Preferences
4. Knowledge of Leisure Opportunities

Specific leisure assessment instruments or scales within instruments will be available in each of the four areas. In general, the Perceived Freedom Short Form and Leisure Preferences should be given as a screening process. If the participant scores low in perceived freedom, the Perceived Freedom Long Form, Barriers to Leisure Involvement, and Knowledge of Leisure Opportunities should be administered to locate leisure difficulties and assist in placement. However, if the participant has no difficulty with perceived freedom, leisure preferences should be matched with the agency's programs. This process could also be computerized using a data-based program, allowing the participant easy and independent access to all the agency's programs which could meet his or her individual needs.

Data Flow Diagrams

This section is included for the reader who has some background in computers and would like to understand the TLASCR more specifically. Data flow diagrams (DFDs) are graphic representations of the TLASCR that logically partition it into its functions and depict it in terms of a flow-of-information, rather than flow-of-control, network. They show the features of the logical system — what it will do — but not the performance of the system — how it will perform its functions. They are multidimensional since a process shown in a higher-level DFD is explored (functionally broken down) in lower-level DFD.

The overall system has four major components (Figure 2):

1. Input (Client), where the participant gives the system information and will in turn receive scores based upon the information submitted;

2. Systems (Trends System), which will administer assessments, send answers to the client file, and give the user's scores via the monitor (viewing screen) or printer (hard copy);

3. File (Client Files), which will store all information provided by the user; and

4. Administrator (Systems Administrator), who will update and inform the system as to the storage placement.

The first DFD (Figure 3) evaluates current leisure level. Level 1.0, Process Client History, provides client history for review. The client provides update-input to process 1.0 and selects the Assess-

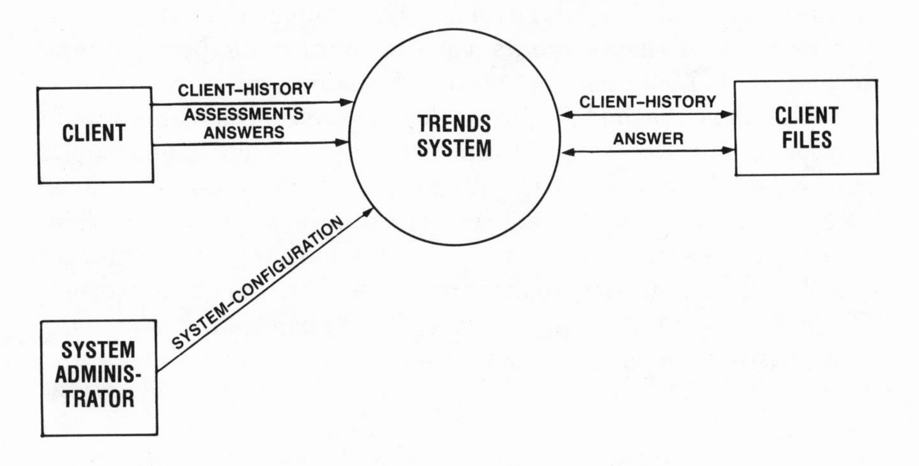

FIG. 2. TRENDS system data flow.

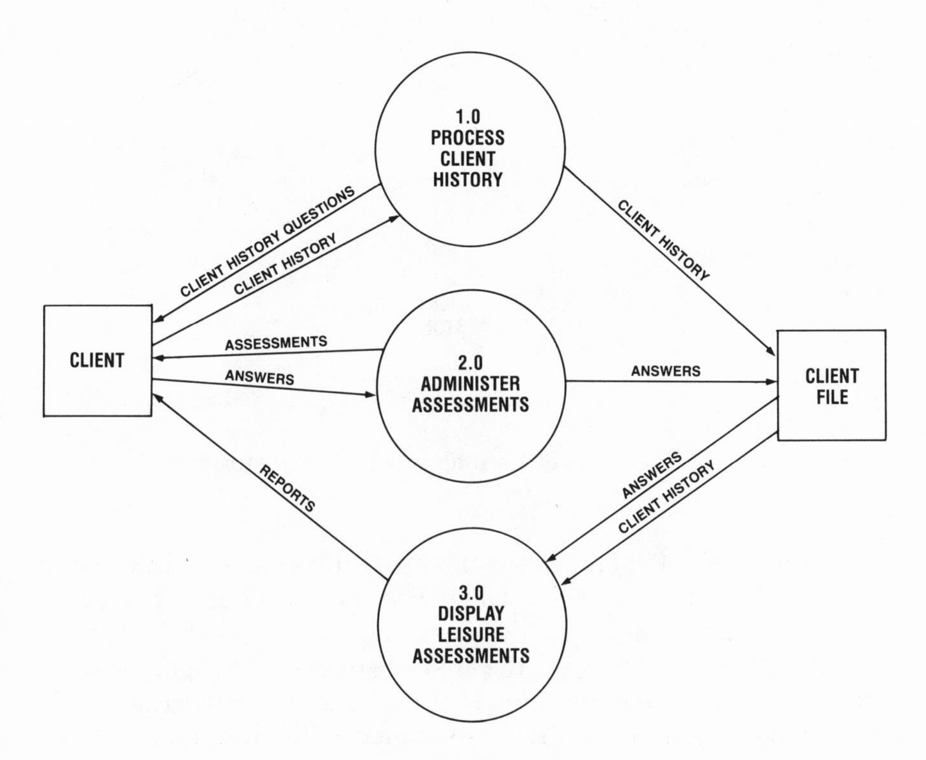

FIG. 3. Level 0. Analysis of TRENDS system.

ments to be administered, Level 2.0. The client can then review the scores of those assessments via the monitor or printed copy through Level 3.0, Display Leisure Assessements.

The level 1.0 DFD (Figure 4) depicts the processes internal to process 1.0 on the 0.0 DFD. Process 1.1., Create Client History, sends client history to the client and receives update-input as well as the various types of client details from the client and/or client background sources. These new client details are sent to process 1.2, Edit Client History, which moves the contents of the Current Client History Store to the Former Client History and writes the new client history to the Current Store.

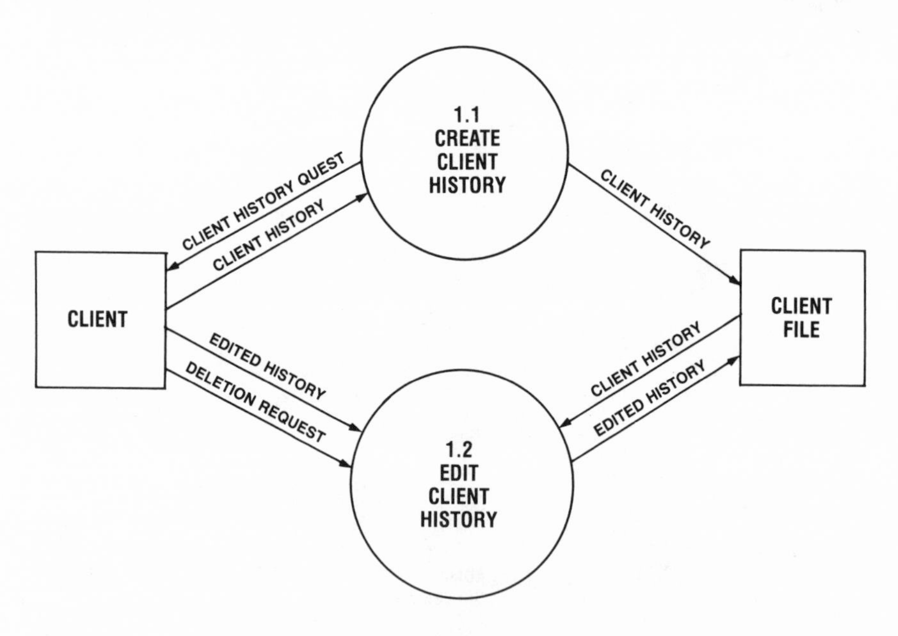

FIG. 4. Level 1. Analysis of client history.

The level 2.0 DFD (Figure 5) shows the processes internal to process 2.0 on the level 0.0 DFD. The 2.1, Administer Perceived Freedom, administers questions associated with either the long or short form and then stores the answers in either the long or short form Perceived Freedom file. The 2.2, Administer Barriers LDB, administers barrier questions associated with scale F and stores the answers in the Barriers Leisure Diagnostic Battery (BLDB) file.

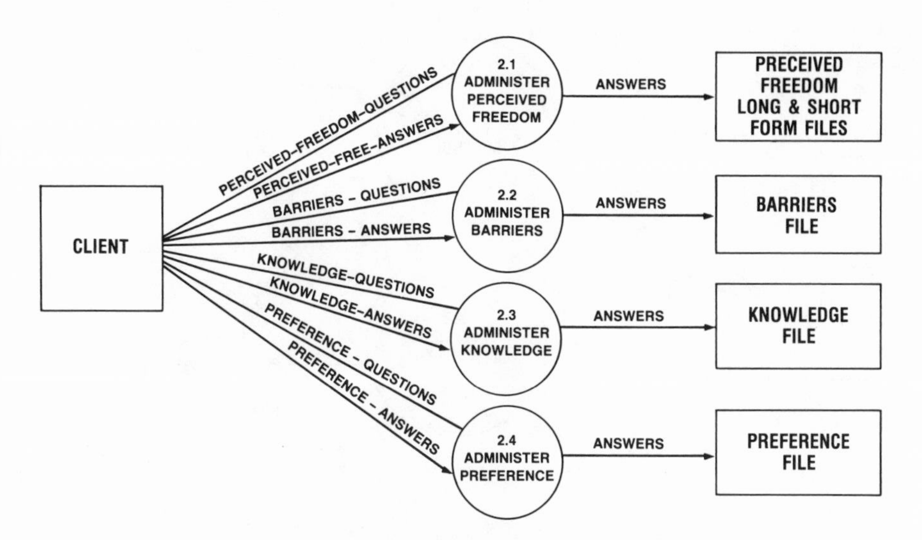

FIG. 5. Level 2. Analysis of administer assessments.

The 2.3, Administer Knowledge, administers the questions associated with scale H from the LDB and then stores the answers in the Knowledge file. Finally the 2.4, Administer Preferences, administers questions associated with scale G from the LDB and then stores the answers in the Preference file.

The level 3.0 DFD (Figure 6) shows the processes internal to process 3.0 on the 0.0 DFD. The 3.1, Print Control, requests via the screen (monitor) the assessment(s) the user wants scored (name and/or date) and how the user wants to receive that information, i.e., on the monitor or printed. The 3.2, Score Assessment, then retrieves the assessment(s) indicated and scores them. Finally the scored assessments are sent to 3.3, Format Report, where the assessment score(s) are formatted and then sent to the screen or printer.

Initial Field Test Results

Initial field testing, which evaluated the effectiveness of selected scales of the TLASCT (i.e., Perceived Freedom Short Form and Leisure Preference scale), has been completed with a university student population (Olsson, Halberg, Edginton, & Chenery, 1987). Using a test-retest method, results indicated that responses to the

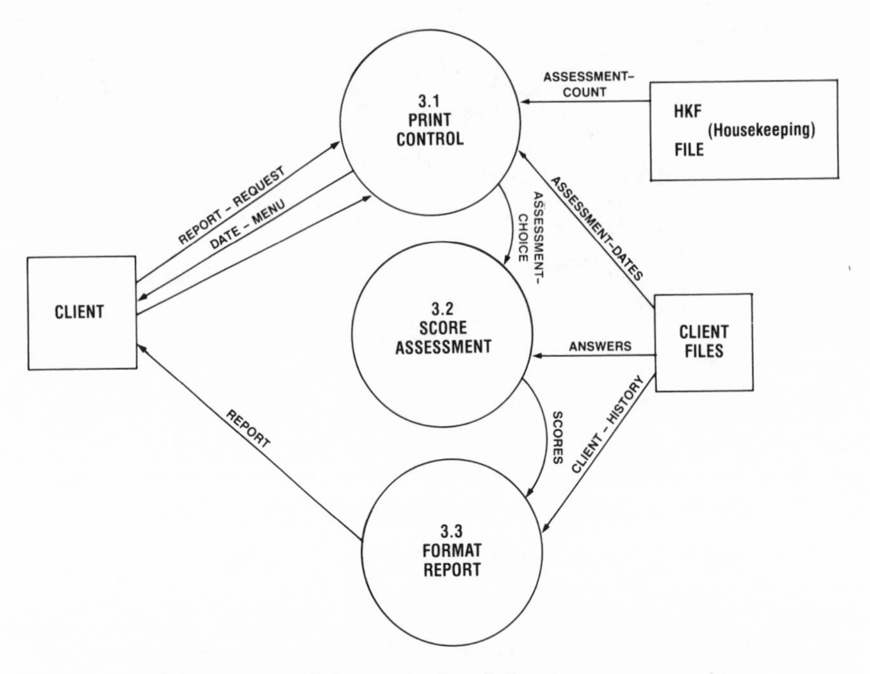

FIG. 6. Level 3. Analysis of display assessments.

selected scales of the automated leisure assessment system were reliable, as were assessment scores obtained manually for the same scales. Subjects had more positive attitudes toward computerized than manual assessment, which was evaluated through a semantic differential-type instrument in response to the stimulus word, assessment. Finally, subjects with little or no microcomputer experience were able to complete and score their assessments independently, given a set of written instructions.

These results, which should be evaluated with some caution, since a university student population may not be comparable to a general community population, suggest that the TLASCR is potentially practical for use by community recreation and park agencies. Since users prefer automated to manual assessment, and individuals were able to complete and score their own assessments independently, use of the system by community recreation agencies could well be cost-effective. Cost-effectiveness can be accomplished since the staff time needed to conduct a leisure assessment component of a program can be considerably reduced as compared with the use of manually completed and scored leisure assessments.

Practical Concerns

1. In order to implement this leisure assessment system and, thus, address individual needs, an agency must have either an Apple II or IBM PC microcomputer. The use of microcomputers by community park and recreation agencies has become relatively common (Stuyt & Siderelis, 1984) and seems likely to increase, considering the continuing decrease in the cost of purchasing them, especially in relationship to their potential for greater efficiency in the management of programs. Microcomputers used during the day for management purposes, such as activity scheduling, word processing, and record keeping, could be used for leisure assessments during the evening hours and on weekends.

2. While the operationalization of the computerized leisure assessment system seems feasible, since initial field test data suggest that individuals using the system can do so independently and have positive attitudes toward automated assessment, the cost of providing such a service might well be questioned. However, it seems possible to offer computerized leisure assessment as an additional service of an agency on a fee basis. People are currently willing to pay a fee for computerized assessments in other areas including nutrition, wellness, fitness, and vocational preferences.

3. Another area of concern may be the necessary staff expertise to adequately interpret the results of the assessment if problems are identified during the independently completed and scored screening process which uses the Perceived Freedom Short Form and the Leisure Preference scale. Should leisure-related problems be identified through the Perceived Freedom Short Form, additional scales could be recommended to more specifically pinpoint the problem(s). These include the original longer version concerned with perceptions of freedom in leisure, which could identify the specific area(s) in which the problem(s) exist, the Barriers to Leisure Experiences scale, and the Knowledge of Leisure Oppotunities scale. If problems are identified, it is recommended that agencies provide qualified professionals to interpret the results and work with the individual to resolve the problem(s), perhaps through leisure education. As was the case with the initial screen-

ing scales, these professionals could be made available through the agency on a fee basis. From the perspective of the need of agencies to limit staff, agencies could contract with professionals for this specialized service (Olsson, Halberg, Edginton, & Chenery, 1987).

CONCLUSIONS

Initial field testing of the assessment system which has been described has been conducted. Once the field test data have been fully evaluated, the Operations Manual and the TLASCR software will be revised as necessary. Future plans include further field testing and examining the three issues listed above with individuals in the community.

All organizations which serve the public (Peters & Waterman, 1982), including leisure service agencies (Grey & Greben, 1974), must develop methods to address individual needs. An inital step which is essential to attempting to meet individual needs is the ability to reliably and efficiently assess leisure needs with some depth on an individual basis. The assessment system described here (TLASCR) should permit community recreation personnel to conduct such an assessment upon which addressing individual needs can be based.

ACKNOWLEDGMENT

Preparation of this article was partially supported by a U.S. Department of Education, Office of Special Education and Rehabilitation Services grant, Project TRENDS, 029EH40018.

REFERENCES

Csikszentmihalyi, M. (1975). *Beyond boredom and anxiety.* San Francisco: Jossey-Bass.

Ellis, G., & Witt, P. (1984). The measurement of perceived freedom in leisure. *Journal of Leisure Research, 16*(2), 110–123.

Gray, E., & Greben (1974). Future perspectives. *California Parks & Recreation,* June/July, 11–19.

Gray, E., & Greben, S. (1982). Future perspectives II: The 1980's and beyond. *Parks & Rrecreation.* May, 52–56.

Iso-Ahola, S. (1980). *The social psychology of leisure and recreation.* Dubuque, IA: William C. Brown.

Lieberman, N. (1977). *Playfulness: Its relationship to imagination and creativity.* New York; Academic Press.

Murphy, J. (1981). *Concepts of leisure: Philosophical implications.* Englewood Cliffs, NJ: Prentice-Hall.

Neulinger, J. (1981). *To leisure, An introduction.* Boston; Allyn & Bacon.

Olsson, R., Halberg, K. J., Edginton, C. E., & Chenary, M. F., (1982). An evaluation of an automated leisure assessment for community-based recreation. *Journal of Park & Recreation Administration. S*(2), 27–39.

Peters, T., & Waterman, R. (1982). *In search of excellence.* New York: Warner Books.

Stuyt, J., & Siderelis, C. (1984). The 1983 national survey of computers in parks and recreation. *Parks and Recreation,* 1984, 19(11), 36–39.

Witt, P., & Ellis, G. (1985). Development of a short form to assess perceived freedom in leisure. *Journal of Leisure Research, 17*(3), 225–233.

Witt, P., & Ellis, G. (1987). *Leisure Diagnostic Battery: Conceptualization, development, reliability, validity, and procedures for testing and scoring.* Denton, TX: North Texas State University.

Witt, P., & Groom R. (1979). Dangers and problems associated with current approaches to developing leisure interest finders. *Therapeutic Recreation Journal, 8*(1), 19–31.

5

RECREATION AND THE RETURNING FEMALE STUDENT

M. Deborah Bialeschki
Karla A. Henderson

Women returning to college after an interruption in their formal education have become quite frequent in colleges and universities today. The purpose of this study was to evaluate the recreation attitudes and recreation participation patterns of a sample of returning female students.

The study was conducted in the fall of 1983 with a random sample of female students at the University of Wisconsin who have returned to graduate school after a five-year lapse in their formal training. Personal interviews were conducted with 36 full-time women students.

The women placed a high value on the cognitive and affective aspects of their recreation activities. However, the scores concerning their behaviorial attitudes were lower indicating that incongruity existed between what the women thought and felt about recreation and what they did in regard to their actual activities.

The greatest barriers to recreation were related to not enough time, work and school being the highest priorities, and too much daily stress. The returning students said they participated less in mass media, social, outdoor, sport, and hobby activities when they returned to school.

The study suggested implications for those who may be programming for women who are returning to school. With the growing number of returning students, traditional student activity and sports programs may not be the best methods for meeting the recreational needs of this group of students.

Women returning to college after an interruption in their formal education have become quite frequent in colleges and universities today. These women often interrupted their schooling because of marriage, due to the need to support husbands completing degrees, for financial reasons, or because they were not encouraged to pursue degree completion (Levine, 1976). While these same factors have influenced many of the women's recreation attitudes and pursuits prior to returning to school, little research has been conducted to determine the changes in women's recreation when they return to school. The purpose of this study was to evaluate the recreation attitudes and recreation participation patterns of a sample of returning female students. The specific research questions were concerned with ascertaining the recreation attitudes of the women, the effect of returning to school on recreation participation, the barriers to recreation, and the relationships of demographic variables to attitudes and participation.

BACKGROUND

Several studies of returning women students have been conducted. The foci of these studies have been the barriers encountered by women returning to school, the reasons why they return, and other such issues. Very few of the studies have directly or indirectly addressed recreation-related issues. A study conducted by Berkove (1977) pointed out that at least half of the women in her study mentioned having "time for myself" as a problem while they were in school. This concern was usually connected to the role strain encountered by the women as well as the guilt associated with putting extra responsibilities on the families (Douvan, 1977). As a consequence, many of the women returning to school gave up some of the "extras" in their lives, such as entertaining and community events (Levine, 1976).

METHODOLOGY

The situational explanation of leisure behavior was selected as the theoretical framework for this study. This framework suggests that recreation behavior is explained by the situation and the environment in which people find themselves. Thus, the recreation behavior of the returning women students would be influenced by the recreation facilities available to the women and the social circle of family and friends. Stover and Garvin's (1982) findings suggest that a change in situation (i.e., returning to school) would produce a change in the recreation behaviors of the women when compared to the behaviors prior to reentering school.

Recreation attitudes of the women were also of interest in this study. The attitude scale designed by Ragheb and Beard was used in this study (Ragheb & Beard, 1982). The only change in the instrument was to replace the word leisure with recreation. This scale measured three components of recreation attitudes:

Cognitive, the basic beliefs of individuals about recreation;
Affective, reflects the liking/disliking of recreation activities;
Behavioral, past present and future intended recreation activities.

The total reliability of the scale is .94, with the three component parts having reliabilities ranging from .89 to .93.

The study was conducted in the fall of 1983 with a random sample of female students at the University of Wisconsin-Madison who had returned to graduate school after at least a five-year lapse in their formal training. The women were chosen randomly from a list supplied by the Graduate Admissions Office of all graduate women in the Colleges of Agriculture and Life Sciences, Education, and Family and Consumer Studues who met the selection criteria. Personal interviews were conducted with 36 full-time students. The interview questions concerned general demographic characteristics, an assessment of recreation attitudes, a listing of barriers to recreation, and an inventory of activities participated in over the past 2 years. Several open-ended questions related to the values of recreation and changes in participation were also asked to provide richness to the quantitative findings.

FINDINGS

The demographic variables were initially analyzed to provide the general background information on this particular sample of returning women students. Table 1 provides the demographic findings from this analysis. The women interviewed had been away from an academic setting for almost 8 years. The average age was 33. Less than half were married and one third of the women had children. Half of the women were currently employed

TABLE 1
Demographic Characteristics of Women Returning to School

Time away from school	8 years
Age	33 years
Marital status	
Married	41%
Not married	59%
Have children	33%
Employed for pay	69%
Total household income	
<$10,000	48%
>$10,001	52%

N = 36

for more than 21 hours a week; 48 percent of the women had a total household income of under $10,000. Approximately 85% of the women were happy about their decision to return to school, whereas the remaining 15% were ambivalent.

The mean scores of the three components of recreation attitudes are found in Table 2. These scores indicated that the women placed a high value on the cognitive and affective aspects of their recreational activities. The means for the cognitive and affective dimensions were 54.6 and 52, respectively, out of a possible 60 points. However, the scores concerning their behavioral attitudes were lower (mean = 43.3). This lower mean indicated that incongruity existed between what the women thought and felt about recreation and what they did in regard to their actual activities. An analysis of variance of these scores and all demongraphic variables indicated that only marital status differed at the .05 significance level. The women who were single placed more importance on the cognitive aspect than did married women (mean = 56.1 and 52.5, respectively). Thus, women who were not married had greater knowledge about recreation and its relationship to the quality of life.

The most highly rated cognitive statements indicated that recreation contributed to one's health, benefited individuals and society, and helped to renew one's energy. The affective state-

TABLE 2
Recreation Attitude Component Scores*

Component	Mean
Cognitive	54.6
Affective	52.0
Behavioral	43.0

*60 points = highest positive attitude component score

ments which were most valued were that recreation was good for an individual, gave pleasure, and was something to be valued. The behavior statements that were rated most highly included that the women would prefer to live in an environment which provides recreation opportunities and, if given a choice, would increase the amount of time spent in recreation, especially if they could afford the time and money.

The next major analysis addressed the situational theoretical suggestion that returning to school would affect the recreation participation of the women students. T-tests were used to analyze the differences in perceived participation levels in mass media recreation, social recreation activities, outdoor activities, sports, cultural activities, and hobbies of the women before and after returning to school. Table 3 contains the before and after recreation participation rates for this sample of women as rated on a Likert scale with 0 = never participate to 6 = participate daily. With the exception of cultural activities, all of the areas showed significant decreases in participation. The greatest meaningful decreases came in the social, mass media, and outdoor activities. The means for mass media (watching television, reading newspapers/magazines, and going to movies) dropped from 1–2 times per week (scale average = 4.2) to about twice a month (scale average = 3.7). Social activities (visiting friends, dancing, parties, etc.) dropped from about twice a month (average = 2.5) to about once a month (average = 1.9). Participation in outdoor activities went from about once a month (average = 1.8) to seldom participating at all (average = 1.3).

When participation rates were analyzed by demographic variables, no differences were found, with the exception of employment level. Women who were employed socialized more than the

TABLE 3
Levels of Recreation Participation of Returning Women Students

	Recreational participation		
Activity	Before return to school	After return to school	*t*-test significance
Mass media	4.2	3.7	.016
Social	2.5	1.9	.002
Outdoor	1.8	1.3	.001
Sport	2.0	1.8	.044
Culture	1.4	1.1	.068
Hobbies	1.4	1.0	.006

*Based on Likert scale with 0 = never do activity to 6 = do daily.

women who were not employed for pay. It was interesting to note that for the entire sample of women, the most frequent recreation activities while in school were reading magazines and newspapers; doing fitness activities, such as swimming, running, and exercising; and watching television.

The remaining area of concern in this study was the barriers to recreation as perceived by these returning women students. The women rated barriers to recreation on a Likert scale with 1 = strongly disagree to 5 = strongly agree. The findings from a general frequencies analysis are found in Table 4. The greatest barriers to recreation for these women were not enough time—work and school being the highest priorities—and too much daily stress. Analysis of variance tests provided no statistically significant differences between barriers and demographic variables.

Several quotes from the open-ended questions provided additional richness from the quantitative findings related to barriers. The problems of reduced time for recreation and, yet, the importance that the women placed on taking time for their own recreation can be illustrated by the following quotes:

> Much less leisure. However, school has forced me to prioritize my leisure; therefore, it's of better quality.

> I've had to plan for it more.

TABLE 4
Top Five Perceived Barriers to Recreation Participation for Returning Women Students

Barrier	Mean*
Not enough time	4.0
School/work main priority	4.0
Too much daily stress	3.7
Recreation commitments hard to maintain	3.3
Not enough money	3.0

*Based on Likert scale with 1 = strongly disagree to 5 = strongly agree.

> I'm impressed with the importance of it. I just couldn't survive without it. I was tense when I first started school; now I allow myself the time and I'm happier for it.

> There is no change in the kinds of activities I do—just less time available for them.

Further analysis of responses from the open-ended questions uncovered an additional conflict for the women. Although they felt that taking time for themselves to participate in recreational activities was important, it also raised feelings of guilt. The following quotes emphasize this dilemma:

> I will occasionally deny myself "my time." However, I can't function for long periods without it.

> I feel guilty about taking time for my leisure. I know leisure is important, so I try to take time.

> Could always be doing something else, so feel more guilty.

It was also important to note that several potential barriers were not seen as deterrents to recreation participation by the women in this study. The women indicated that not knowing what was available to do, not knowing what to select, and not having the skills or the proper fitness levels were not inhibiting factors.

CONCLUSIONS

This study found that although women's attitudes toward recreation were indeed positive, their recreation patterns were adversely affected by their return to academia. These outcomes would support the findings from Stover and Garbin's (1982) study of the situational hypothesis of leisure that states that the environment rather than personal characteristics influence the individual's behaviors. While the women's cognitive and affective dimensions of leisure were quite positive, the actual behaviors were considerably lower. This fact indicated a discrepancy between perception and action on the part of these women returning to graduate school.

The qualitative data from the study provide a possible means for better understanding the impact of the change of situation on women's lives. Although more women are returning to school, they still must contend with the sex role expectations and socialization that occurs in our society. This socialization emphasizes the primacy of women's role's to home and family concerns. Women are socialized to put others, particularly family, before themselves. If they violate this sex role expectation by placing their needs first, guilt often follows. In this study, returning women students may have felt forced to decrease their personal recreation behaviors as a means for lessening the internal role conflicts, even though they had positive attitudes toward recreation. These women may have sacrificed to some degree their own recreation in order to maintain time for significant others or to meet family obligations. Perhaps the interaction between situational and socialization theories of leisure needs to be further explored, with the critical factor in socialization theory being the socialization to sex role expectations that affect recreation behaviors rather than the socialization of the individual to particular activities.

Several conclusions and considerations for professionals programming in university as well as community recreation can be suggested. Since women continued to be involved in fitness-oriented activities, having university facilities and organized programs accessible to them while at school would be a consideration. Returning to school did lessen the actual amount of time spent participating in activities, but the value the subjects placed on their recreation remained high. Since past research has indicated that women feel guilty about taking time for themselves, offering family-oriented activities or providing childcare at the recreational site may be other alternatives to consider.

With the growing number of returning students, traditional student activities and sports programs may not be the best methods for meeting the recreational needs of this group of students. Recreation planners need to consider offering programs throughout the day, especially fitness activities. It is clear from the women's responses that recreation is an integral part of their lives, and that ways to meet their recreational needs are important to consider.

REFERENCES

Berkove, G. (1977). Returning women students: A study of stress and success. *The Newsletter, 10*(1), 5, Center for Continuing Education for Women, University of Michigan.

Douvan, E. (1977) Researchers talk about problems of women's continuing education. *The Newsletter, 10*(1), 1–4, 8, Center for Continuing Education of Women, University of Michigan.

Levine, A. (1976). Between the stages of life: Adult women on a college scene. *Educational Horizons,* pp. 154–161.

Ragheb, M. & Beard, J. (1982). Measuring leisure attitudes. *Journal of Leisure Research, 14*(2); 156–167.

Stover, R., & Garbin, A. (1982) Explanations of leisure behavior: An analysis. *Journal of Leisure Research, 14*(2), 91–99.

6

CHICAGO STEELWORKER LAYOFFS: UNEMPLOYMENT AND LIFE AND LEISURE SATISFACTION

Lisa C. Pesavento Raymond

The purpose of this study was to examine the effects of unemployment on the life and leisure satisfaction of unemployed steelworkers. The study population was drawn from Republic Steel's union facility site, Local 1033, located on the southeast side of Chicago. Survey development followed Depression studies and solicited selected demographic and behavioral characteristics along with self-reported changes pertaining to life and leisure satisfaction. Analyses consisted of: (1) descriptive statistics for 20 statements measuring life and leisure satisfaction both before and after unemployment; (2) cross tabluations of before unemployment leisure satisfaction on after unemployment life satisfaction; and (3) analyses of variance of change in life and leisure satisfaction scale scores by sex, race, age, marital status, length of unemployment, and financial buffers. Results showed that respondents indicated a slight drop in both their life and leisure satisfaction after unemployment. Marital status and age were significantly related to the change in leisure satisfaction ($p < .05$*). Over 66% of the respondents had high levels of both leisure and life satisfaction, and only 33% did when unemployed, a decrease of 50%. Those who more highly satisfied were more likely to reflect a change (decrease) after unemployment.*

A dramatic increase in unemployment of the American working class took place in the 1980s. Blue-collar positions were hit hard by temporary job shutdowns and permanent plant closings early in the decade. In 1980, for example, one-fourth of all workers in blue-collar occupations were unemployed for at least 1 week, the highest among all occupational groups. In contrast, only one-tenth of white-collar workers encountered some unemployment during the year (Terry, 1982). The Labor Department reported that unemployment matched a postwar high of 10.8% in December 1982, and Illinois' jobless rolls swelled to 13.2%. It was also noted that joblessness for adult males reached 10.1%, surpassing the earlier record; unemployment among blacks soared to a record 20.5%, and the number of Americans who had been jobless for 3 months or more increased, leaving many without extended unemployment benefits because of the 1981 budget cuts (Bureau of Labor Statistics, July, 1983). In October 1982, the mean duration of unemployment was 17.2 weeks. It was becoming increasingly evident that the average working-class American was experiencing a decrease in employment stability.

Unemployment and its impact on life and leisure satisfaction became pertinent issues with the dramatic increase in unemployment of the American working class. The purpose of this study was to examine the effects of unemployment on the life and leisure satisfaction of unemployed steelworkers. No North American research has measured this relationship since the 1950s. A number of studies, which were carried out during the Depression of the 1930s and the auto plant closings of the 1950s, examined working-class families' reactions to unemployment and lowered income. The early work of Komarovsky (1940) and Bakke (1940) indicated that the longer the unemployment experience lasted, the more drastically leisure was curtailed. Leisure satisfaction appeared to change, if not somewhat disintegrate, under the impact of the necessary adjustments to unemployment during the Depression. Literature of the 1930s and 1950s indicated that unemployment also had substantial deleterious effects on overall life satisfaction. (Bakke, 1940; Wilcock & Franke, 1963).

A number of recent British studies have assessed proposed areas of research in unemployment and leisure (Smith & Simpkins, 1980) and examined the objectives and outcomes of leisure provision for the unemployed (Glyptis, 1983; Kay, 1984). Smith and Simpkins (1980) suggested that sociological and psychological research within systematic frameworks of analyses needed to be done. Further, positive policy strategies and evaluative programs needed to be established which recognized the psychologically crippling effect of unemployment and which aided in the development of personal worth and social resourcefulness. Glyptis (1983), in her evaluation of British (Leicester and Birmingham) government-sponsored sport schemes, found that program success depended largely on a number of factors, including well-organized central administrations with necessary support staffs, location of services in small-scale local centers, and the placement of sports leaders as community workers. Kay (1984), also affiliated with the Leicester and Birmingham schemes, echoed the findings of Glyptis and argued that sport had its limitations and that it did not appeal universally to all unemployed participants. She indicated that the programs also needed to be protected from disruptions in scheduling and must be especially sensitive to the needs of the unemployed.

Recent North American studies have evaluated the psychological and physical effects of unemployment on individuals and their families (Rayman, 1983; Perfetti & Bingham, 1983), yet have not addressed the issues of life and leisure satisfaction. Rayman's (1983) policy considerations based on an extensive review of research dealing with the social and private costs of unemployment were insightful. She states that, although unemployed workers and their families turned to close relatives for help, they were generally unfamiliar with community agencies that could be of service to them. She cautioned against concluding that unemployment inevitably impaired mental and physical health. However, Perfetti and Bingham (1983) found that unemployed workers scored lower on measures of self-esteem than employed workers and noted the self-blaming behavior that seemed to be associated with reduced self-esteem and the disruptive effects of unemployment on family relationships.

Raymond (1984) reported the effects of length of unemployment on activity, leisure expenditure, and family leisure. Generally, leisure activity participation decreased and cost was perceived as a greater problem for those activities in which participation decreased. Companionship, or whom the individuals did the activities with—alone, with family or friends—tended to depend upon the activity.

This current study extends Raymond's previous research with

steelworkers to examine life and leisure satisfaction as influenced by unemployment. The specific objectives were answers to the following questions:

1. What are the general levels of life and leisure satisfaction both before and after unemployment?
2. How does the level of life satisfaction before unemployment relate to the level of life satisfaction after unemployment?
3. How does the level of leisure satisfaction before unemployment relate to the level of leisure satisfaction after unemployment?
4. How are demographic variables related to change in both life and leisure satisfaction?
5. How does level of leisure satisfaction before unemployment relate to level of life satisfaction before unemployment?
6. How does level of leisure satisfaction after unemployment relate to level of life satisfaction after unemployment?

METHOD

Site Negotiation

Selection of an appropriate site proved to be one of the greatest challenges of the study. Many of the largest and most recent layoffs of steelworkers have been from manufacturing and steel production industries located in urban locales, such as Chicago and surrounding suburbs. A reluctance on the part of management of several steel companies to release the names and addresses of potential survey participants forced the investigator to seek out the leaders of the unions within the companies for assistance. Although the union leaders also refused to provide names and addresses of the laid-off workers, they did offer the investigator access to various union halls and cooperation from the nonworking ranks. However, an inability of Wisconsin Steel and U.S. Steel union halls to yield an adequate number of study participants prevented their union members from participating in the study at those sites.

For those reasons, the study population was drawn from Republic Steel's union facility site on the southeast side of Chicago.

Union Local 1033 had a leadership that was highly cooperative and had over 3,000 people out of work. According to union calculations, one half of the inactive workers were believed to be on permanent layoff. The majority of the unemployed had been given no more than one week's notice prior to being released from their jobs. Members varied widely across skill categories, from electricians to carpenters and welders to millwrights and janitors.

Negotiating a site also included assurances that the union leadership required. The investigator had to present the proposed study to the President of 1033 and the Unemployment Committee, a board which regulated activities for the unemployed of the local. After reviewing the testing instrument and the objectives of the study, permission was granted to distribute the questionnaire. Assurance was also given that anonymity would be observed, and no one would be pressured to participate by the investigator.

Selection of time for questionnaire administration adhered to three peak periods when the facililty was in use by the largest number of unemployed steelworkers. On the third Thursday of each month, unemployed 1033 members participated in a food giveaway program which was coordinated by the Unemployment Committee. Approximately 100 people came to the facility each month to pick up a thirty-dollar bag of groceries distributed one to a family. The second period utilized was the first week of each month, designated as a sign-up week for the giveaway program. People were not allowed to pick up food unless they had signed up 2 weeks earlier. This allowed for an orderly distribution and for strictly kept records. The third period was on Mondays, when the Illinois Unemployment Bureau used the 1033 union facility as a branch site. The facility was then fully staffed with Bureau workers and served 50 to 100 people, many of whom were unemployed 1033 members. At this period, subjects did not necessarily belong to Local 1033 but included unemployed steelworkers from other locals. It was decided that all steelworkers unemployed for at least one month who visited the research site at the selected times would be included in the study, regardless of their union affiliation. This group would serve as a source of additional participants to those of Local 1033 and would be treated as one group if shown to be homogeneous.

Sample Parameters

The primary requirements for the sample were (1) steelworker as occupation and (2) unemployed for at least one month. The location brought together short- and long-term unemployed individuals whose unemployment ranged from 1 month to 36 months. The layoff period needed to be long enough to have affected older workers and those without children living at home. A sample was needed which would exhibit a range of age and stage within the life cycle. Older personnel with seniority advantage were included. Participants were not randomly selected since they needed to be screened to meet the study criteria. Because randomization was not possible, this study did not attempt to generalize beyond the sample. Due to the length and complexity of the questionnaire, it was necessary for the investigator to be present to aid in giving directions and answering questions. No predetermined sample size was set since it was not known how cooperative the population would be. The investigator expected to stay as long as the three Mondays, 3 food sign-ups, and 3 food giveaways extending from June 10, 1983, to September 5, 1983.

Limitations of the Sample

Every attempt was made to be as inclusive as possible of all persons who entered the 1033 facility. However, because of the nonrandom sampling of those who came to the facility, there was no way of knowing who the study population did not include. It was not possible to establish whether the study population was representative of unemployed steelworkers in general, of those who came to the facility, or of those who were members of Local 1033. Individuals who were too depressed, too busy, or had unreported jobs may have been missed.

Development of Instrument

Survey development followed the Depression studies and solicited selected demographic and behavioral characteristics along with self-reported changes pertaining to life and leisure satisfaction. Statements 1–15, dealing with leisure satisfaction, were adapted for the questionnaire from Beard and Ragheb's (1980)

Leisure Satisfaction Scale and attempted to determine the degree of leisure salience before unemployment and the change that occurred after unemployment. With limited questionnaire space and participant time considerations, an effort was made to include as many of Beard and Ragheb's leisure satisfaction domains as possible (psychological, physiological, etc.) and also to include a number of family, friends, home, and activity related statements common to this particular blue-collar sample. Selection responses in a Likert-type recall format ranged from: SD = strongly disagree, D = disagree, N = neutral, A = agree, and SA = strongly agree. An instrument format example follows:

Before Unemployment		After Unemployment
SA A N D SD	1. The most satisfying things that happen to me involve leisure activities with my family.	SA A N D SD
SA A N D SD	2. My leisure activities give me a feeling of accomplishment.	SA A N D SD

A five–item life satisfaction scale taken from Quinn and Staines's (1979) Quality of Employment Survey served as the model for obtaining the life satisfaction scores. Respondents were asked to answer statements 16–20 as they would have before they were unemployed and after being unemployed. An instrument example follows:

Before Unemployment		After Unemployment
SA A N D SD	16. I am satisfied with my life as a whole.	SA A N D SD
SA A N D SD	17. All in all, there is a good deal of happiness in my life.	SA A N D SD

A suitable method of measuring data was required for this small scale and limited resource project. Since measuring change based on recall may have been unreliable for an individual, it was decided that numerically recalling frequency or degree of change would be less accurate and less consistent than with a Likert-type scale. A selected method of measuring change without numbers was utilized successfully by Wilcock and Franke (1963) and Aiken, Ferman, and Sheppard (1968) and was adapted for this study. The author was aware of the probable direction of memory bias that may have distorted past attitudes into agreement with present ones. However, until longitudinal research is available the current data must be considered exploratory in its contribution and regarded with proper caution (Campbell & Stanley, 1966).

Administration of the Instrument

As mentioned in the Sample Parameters section, the instrument was administered during three time periods which extended from June 10, 1983, to September 5, 1983. The investigator was present for 3 food sign-ups, 3 food giveaways, and 13 branch unemployment Mondays. During all three periods, participants had access to seating and pencils in a well-lighted room. The purpose of the survey and the procedures to be followed in filling out the form were explained, and each person was allowed to fill out the instrument at his or her own pace. The researcher was available to supervise, to answer questions, and to assist those who had difficulty in filling out the questionnaire.

There were no means by which to assess the bias that may have occurred for the individuals who did or did not fill out the questionnaires because of the sex and appearance of the investigator. Every attempt was made to conform to the dress of those who entered the facility. The investigator endeavored to develop a level of trust with the respondents from Local 1033 by assembling and distributing the food packages. The volunteer efforts in assisting the Unemployment Committee were acknowledged and appreciated. Both the President and the Unemployment Committe sanctioned the presence of the investigator over the 3-month period. However, it was not possible to determine what, if any, bias was present.

DATA ANALYSIS

The analyses consisted of:

1. Descriptive statistics for the 20 statements measuring life and leisure satisfaction both before and after unemployment. Scale scores measuring change were formed for each of the respondents by taking the mean for each respondent over all of the 15 leisure statements, once for the before and once for the after unemployment responses. The same procedure was utilized over all five life satisfaction statements. Scores ranged from 1.00 (strongly disagree) to 5.00 (strongly agree).
2. Cross tabulations of before-unemployment leisure satisfaction on after-unemployment leisure satisfaction. Cross tabulations, or contingency tables, were used to indicate the joint frequency distribution of cases according to two or more classification variables. The joint frequency distributions were statistically analyzed by a chi-square statistic, or test of significance. The strength of the associations were then measured by the appropriate lambda or gamma statistic. The variables were formed by collapsing the responses from the 15 leisure and five life satisfaction statements for each respondent to include: <1> 1.00 – 2.80 = low satisfaction, <2> 2.801–3.80 = medium satisfaction, and <3> 3.801–5.00 = high satisfaction, for both the before-and after- unemployment categories. This was done by separating the response averages after examining the frequency distribution.
3. Analyses of variance of change in life and leisure satisfaction scale scores (formed by taking the after scale score minus the before scale score) by sex, race, age, marital status, length of unemployment, and financial buffers. It was determined that an analysis of variance using a number of pertinent demographic variables would also provide additional insight in the attempt to identify any influential independent variables. This procedure was used due to the nominal and ordinal nature of the demographic variables. Even though there was a greater likelihood of finding significant relationships when doing sev-

eral analyses of variance, the exploratory nature of the study indicated the need to examine differences in leisure behavior patterns as a function of each demographic variable treated in a invariate fashion. Tukey procedures were then applied to identify pairs of means significantly different at the .05 level (Glass & Stanley, 1970). Therefore, the method of analyses included cross tabulation and a series of analyses of variance in order to examine relationships among variables.

RESULTS

The sample for this study consisted of 240 unemployed steelworkers, the majority of whom were Local 1033 members. Local 65 and other affiliations were also represented. Seven individuals indicated that they did not wish to participate in the study because of the time it would take to fill out the questionnaire. An additional 19 were primarily Spanish speaking and could not participate because they did not read or write English sufficiently to complete the questions. Eight questionnaires were not filled out completely and, therefore, were not included in the sample.

The length of time laid off ranged from 1 month to 36 months. The majority of respondents, 58.7%, were married, 25.4% were never married, and 15.9% were divorced, widowed, or separated. Of the sample, 83.3% were Caucasian, 15.4% were black; and 1.2% did not report a racial background. Thirteen percent of the total sample indicated that they were of Hispanic descent. Eighty-four percent were male, and the mean age was 35. Ninety-four percent were unemployed and seeking work, and 4.6% were employed part-time and seeking work. The educational level of the sample showed 52.1% were high school graduates and 30.4% had some college education. In 1982, over half of the respondents had total household incomes between $10,000 and $14,000.

Respondents indicated that there was a slight drop in both life and leisure satisfaction levels after unemployment. The before-unemployment mean, 3.78, indicated a level of agreement with the statements measuring life satisfaction. The after-unemployment mean, 2.82, indicated a .96 drop, or a response level between disagreement and neutrality. Respondents showed that there was a drop of almost one measurement unit in their life satisfaction after unemployment. The before-unemployment mean, 3.77, indicated a level of agreement with the statements measuring leisure satisfaction. The after-unemployment mean, 3.40, indicated a .37 drop or a response level between neutrality and agreement.

Level of life satisfaction before unemployment was significantly related to the level of life satisfaction after unemployment (see Table 1). The chi-square was significant ($p<.01$), while the gamma value was .244. The contingency table differentiated by level in that 76% of the respondents who indicated a low level of satisfaction before unemployment remained at that level after unemployment. Of those who indicated a medium level of satisfaction after, and 28% of the respondents who were at a high level prior to unemployment showed a level of low satisfaction after unemployment. Therefore, while level of life satisfaction before unemployment was significantly related to the level of life satisfaction after unemployment, it appeared to be different for those more or less satisfied.

Level of leisure satisfaction before unemployment was significantly related to the level of leisure satisfaction after unemployment (See Table 1). The chi-square was significant ($p<.01$), whereas the gamma value was .396. The contingency table differentiated by levels in that of the respondents who indicated a low level of satisfaction before unemployment, 69% remained at that level after unemployment. Of those who indicated a medium level of satisfaction, 80% had the same level after, and of those who were at a high level prior to unemployment, 45% showed a level of high satisfaction after unemployment.

Of the demographic variables analyzed, none was significantly related to the change in life satisfaction whereas marital status and age were significantly related to the change in leisure satisfaction ($p<.05$). The Tukey procedure indicated that there was a statistically significant difference between the means of the married and never-married groups. The married respondents, with a mean of .48, had a greater drop in leisure satisfaction level after unemployment than the never married respondents at .11. The Tukey procedure, computed on leisure satisfaction for age, denoted a statistically significant difference between the 20–29 and 40–49 age groups. The 40–49 age group, with a mean of .62, had a greater drop in leisure satisfaction level after unemployment than the 20–29 age group at .21.

TABLE 1
Frequencies (percentages), Significance Levels, and Gamma Values for Crosstabulations of Life and Leisure Satisfaction Scores Before and After Unemployment

Variable				
Life satisfaction	Life Satisfaction After Unemployment			
before unemployment**	low	med	high	total
low	22(75.9)[a]	6(20.7)[a]	1(3.4)[a]	29(12.3)[a]
medium	35(38.9)	54(60.0)	1(1.1)	90(38.3)
high	58(50.0)	25(21.6)	33(28.4)	116(49.4)
total	115(48.9)	85(36.2)	35(14.9)	235(100.0)
gamma .244				
Leisure satisfaction	Life Satisfaction After Unemployment			
before unemployment**	low	med	high	total
low	9(69.2)	1(7.7)	3(23.1)	13(5.5)
medium	12(11.3)	85(80.2)	9(8.5)	106(45.1)
high	24(20.7)	4(34.5)	52(44.8)	116(49.4)
total	45(19.1)	126(53.6)	64(27.2)	235(100.0)
gamma .396				
Leisure satisfaction	Life Satisfaction Before Unemployment			
before unemployment**	low	med	high	total
low	8(61.5)	3(23.1)	2(15.4)	13(5.5)
medium	14(13.2)	54(50.9)	38(35.8)	106(45.1)
high	7(6.0)	33(28.4)	76(65.5)	116(49.4)
total	29(12.3)	90(38.3)	116(49.4)	235(100.0)
gamma .553				
Leisure satisfaction	Life Satisfaction After Unemployment			
after unemployment**	low	med	high	total
low	49(93.3)	2(4.4)	1(2.2)	45(19.1)
medium	56(44.4)	57(45.2)	13(10.3)	126(53.6)
high	17(26.6)	26(40.6)	21(32.8)	64(27.2)
total	115(48.9)	85(36.2)	35(14.9)	235(100.0)
gamma .656				

[a]percentages, ** $p < .01$.

Level of leisure satisfaction before unemployment was significantly related to level of life satisfaction before unemployment (see Table 1). The chi-square was significant at the .01 level, and the gamma value was .553. The contingency table differentiated by levels in that of the respondents who indicated a low level of leisure satisfaction before unemployment, 62% had a low level of life satisfaction. Of those who had a medium level of leisure satisfaction, 51% had a medium level of life satisfaction, and of those who were at a high level of leisure satisfaction, 66% were also at a high level of life satisfaction before.

Level of leisure satisfaction after unemployment was significantly related to the level of life satisfaction after unemployment (see Table 1). The chi-square was significant at the .01 level, and the gamma value was .656. The contingency table differentiated by levels in that of the respondents who indicated a low level of leisure satisfaction after unemployment, 93% had a low level of life satisfaction. Of those who had a medium level of leisure satisfaction, 45% had a medium level of life satisfaction, and of those who were at a high level of leisure satisfaction, 33% were also at a high level of life satisfaction after. Before unemployment, over 66% of the respondents had high levels of both leisure and life satisfaction, and only 33% did when unemployed, a decrease of 50%. Those who were highly satisfied before were more likely to reflect a change (decrease) after unemployment. Fewer respondents indicated a change from high levels of leisure satisfaction to lower levels after unemployment. But comparing the relationship between leisure and life satisfaction before unemployment to that of after unemployment, it was clear that the overall relationship between the two remained quite high.

DISCUSSION

The findings indicated that the overall decline of life and leisure satisfaction was slight. Although difficult to compare accurately, this sample did not demonstrate the radical decrease in leisure satisfaction that appeared to occur during the Depression. Bakke (1940) and Komarovsky (1940) reported that leisure was dissatisfying after the loss of work, but did not measure this attitude change directly. Komarovsky stated that the leisure of the unemployed individual was so filled with economic privations, anxiety, and humiliation that it was quite different from the leisure of the employed. Unemployment greatly reduced feelings of self-respect and self-worth.

A number of new or secondary factors may have had an impact on leisure satisfaction after unemployment for this sample. With more education than those during the 1930s, individuals had greater exposure to a variety of activities. The current sample also had access to more opportunities and resources, and access to transportation was readily available as was in-home television. Both public and private recreation opportunities have increased in availability. With increased variety came the possibility of selecting from activities of both high and low cost. It may have been possible to choose alternate activities and not just discontinue activities. Leisure satisfaction may not have been significantly diminished since all leisure activity was not discontinued or radically decreased as it was over 50 years ago.

Financial buffering was generally present for the individuals in this study. Over half of the sample had at least one form of financial buffer through a spouse working, unemployment compensation, or other income. Consequently, financial resource depletion because of extended unemployment may not have posed the same obstacle for this sample as it did for those at the time of the Depression.

Other attitudinal changes have taken place since the 1930s and may have influenced leisure behavior adaptation. In conversations with the individuals in the sample, it was indicated that unemployment compensation was viewed as a right and not as charity. There was a certain confidence that old jobs would again be available and that it was only a matter of time. Today's family may also have been somewhat more egalitarian in its functioning and the potential for a diverse income base was also increased. Through these buffering mechanisms, the sample may have been capable of maintaining continuity in their leisure which allowed for satisfaction to remain relatively unchanged.

CONCLUSIONS

The positive contribution to quality of life that leisure can make must be considered. The current findings showed that though the level of life satisfaction dropped considerably after unemployment, leisure satisfaction did not show as much decline. Leisure cannot be seen as a replacement for work, yet may have an important role to play in the lives of the unemployed. Role and identity losses impact on self-definition. Any engagement which provides for positive self-definition should be supported. Leisure may serve as a comfortable setting for self-expression. Educating for leisure may also provide the necessary tools for coping with "time on one's hands" and the boredom that accompanies loss of work—issues frequently highlighted by conversations with the sample.

Existing public and private facilities must be utilized for maximum effectiveness within the community. Nonprime time recreation scheduling can be adapted to coincide with the more flexible hours of those out of work. The focus should shift to what will be acceptable to individuals who have a reduced ability to pay. This may entail provisions for the opportunity to participate at reduced cost prices at off-hour times of the day. Awareness of what is available can be advertised through the local churches, union halls, and unemployment offices. Above all, an atmosphere of support which allows for leisure choices to be made needs to be encouraged. With respect to future research, leisure may well be studied as a coping tool for unemployment and a contributor to life satisfaction.

REFERENCES

Aiken, M., Ferman, L. A., & Sheppard, H. L. (1968). *Economic failure, alienation and extremism.* Ann Arbor: University of Michigan Press.

Bakke, W. E. (1940). *Citizens without work: A study of unemployment upon the workers' social relations and practices.* New Haven: Yale University Press.

Beard, J. G., & Ragheb, M. G. (1980). Measuring leisure satisfaction. *Journal of Leisure Research,* 12 (1); 20–33. Bureau of labor statistics. (1983). *Monthly Labor Review, 106* (7), 49–87.

Campbell, D. T., & Stanley, J. C. (1966). *Experimental and quasi-experimental designs for research.* Chicago: Rand McNally College Publishing.

Glass, G. V., & Stanley, J. C. (1970). *Statistical methods in education and psychology.* Englewood Cliffs, NJ: Prentice-Hall.

Glyptis, S. (1983). Business as usual? Leisure provision for the unemployed. *Leisure Studies,* 2(3), 287–300.

Hargreaves, D. H. (1981). Unemployment, leisure and education. *Oxford Review of Education,* 7(3), 197–209.

Jahoda, M. (1982). *Employment and unemployment: A social-psychological analysis.* London: Cambridge University Press.

Kay, T. (1984). Leisure provision for the unemployed: Objectives and achievements. Paper presented at the Congress of the World Leisure and Recreation Association, Marly-le-Roi, France.

Komarovsky, M. (1940). *The unemployed man and his family: The effect of unemployment upon the status of the man in fifty-nine families.* New York: Dryden Press.

Perfetti, L., & Bingham, C. (1983). Unemployment and self-esteem in metal refinery workers. *Vocational Guidance Quarterly, 1*(3), 195–202.

Quinn, R. P., & Staines, G. L. (1977). *The 1977 quality of employment survey.* Ann Arbor: University of Michigan Research Center.

Rayman, P. (1983). The human and social costs of unemployment. Paper presented at the Congressional Seminar of the Consortium of Social Science Associations, Washington, D. C.

Raymond, L. C. Pesavento, (1984). The effects of unemployment on the leisure behavior of unemployed steelworkers. *World Leisure and Recreation, 26*(5), 61–64.

Smith, M., & Simpkins, N. (1980). *Unemployment and leisure: A review and some proposals for research.* University of Salford, UK: The Center for Leisure Studies.

Terry, S. L. (1982). Unemployment and its effect on family income in 1980. *Monthly Labor Review, 105*(4), 35–43.

Wilcock, R. C., & Franke, W. H. (1963). *Unwanted workers: Permanent layoffs and long-term unemployment*. Glencoe, IL: Free Press of Glencoe.

7

THE THERAPEUTIC RECREATION PROFESSIONAL AS BEHAVIOR CONTROL AGENT

Miriam Lahey

This paper reports on selected findings of a 1985/86 study of 150 New York nursing home residents and 50 therapeutic recreation professionals serving in long-term care institutions. The study explored congruence of resident and therapeutic recreation staff perception of the influence of both positive and negative reinforcers on participation in the nursing home recreation programs.

In addition, the therapeutic recreation staff were asked about their willingness as professionals to promote participation in their programs through the active use of reinforcers and to indicate items which they perceived as rewards for their professional service.

The study found considerable difference between resident and staff perceptions of motivators for resident participation. Furthermore, staff seemed to be unaware of the strength of their influence on resident behavior. This paper reflects upon the implication of these findings for both nursing home residents and the therapeutic recreation staff. It recommends further research along these lines and rigorous training in behavior control for all therapeutic recreation professionals.

Although there is a growing body of literature describing the use of behavioral modification methods in the general treatment of emotional and physical illness, there has been little attempt to assess such methods as they operate in long-term care institutions serving the elderly. For the most part, management and staff in nursing homes do not seem to be aware of the behavior control practiced in their facilities.

The literature on behavioral modification suggests, however, that nursing homes provide a climate in which behavioral control can flourish. Goffman (1961) includes nursing homes among "total institutions" whose residents he sees as particularly vulnerable to behavior control. Skinner (1976), in turn, describes the powerful reinforcers which can operate within the nursing home environment. He notes, for example, that the guarantee of certain absolutes—food, shelter, clothing—can reverse the normal effect such stimuli have when they are contingent upon individual action. Because the institutionalized elderly need do nothing for food, medical care, and other needs, these traditional reinforcers of positive, active behavior may become reinforcers of passivity and dependency.

Furthermore, when normally contingent reinforcers of behavior become absolutized, it is likely, according to Skinner, that other, lesser, contingent reinforcers will take over. In other words, throughout their lives, nursing home residents have had to make some effort or to behave in certain ways in order to secure their livelihood or obtain other rewards. Now, in the nursing home, many of their basic needs are absolutely guaranteed. Without anyone realizing what is happening, objects which seem motivationally paltry in a resident's life can begin to claim all the motivating power once levied by the struggle for sustenance, for professional/economic advancement, for the care and nurturing of family members. As a consequence, the institutional environment can effectively diminish or trivialize the residents behavioral repertoires, radically shifting behavioral reinforcers, so that accidental contingencies may become as powerful as planned ones.

Because of the immense reinforcement potential of such contingencies, it is important to recognize their operation in all departments of the long-term care institution. Such awareness is of particular importance for recreation professionals who provide one of the few services in which the client's free choice and control are critical factors.

Underlying philosophies vary as to the optimal degree of client autonomy, or free choice, in therapeutic recreation. Peterson and Gunn (1984) describe therapeutic recreation service as ranging along a continuum. At one end, the staff has total control. Thus, therapeutic recreation professionals supporting a prescriptive model of service argue that clients requiring intervention for habilitation or rehabilitation are not capable of choosing their own leisure pursuits (Kraus, 1984). At the other end of the continuum, however, client autonomy is quite primary. Thus McDowell (1986) notes recent challenges to the "Leisure Ability" philosophy. For example, some (Sylvester, 1985; Mobily, 1985; Hunnicutt, 1980) are concerned about the controlling behaviors of therapeutic recreation professionals as they attempt to "induce the leisure experience in their clients" (McDowell, 1986, p. 29).

In line with such expressions of concern, this paper focuses on the nature and extent of the control exercised by therapeutic recreation professionals serving the elderly in nursing homes and on the degree to which both staff and clients are aware of such control. Since these clients are particularly likely to be seen as "frozen" at a diminished level of competence (Schmidt, 1982; Baltes, Burgess, & Stewart, 1980), there may be a corresponding tendency for staff-members to keep them at that lower end of the therapeutic recreation continuum where the institution has full control.

In brief, then, nursing home residents are particularly vulnerable to control by professionals. Moreover, therapeutic recreation philosophy does not always provide the professional with clear, unambiguous guidelines concerning client autonomy (Halberg & Howe-Murphy, 1985). In addition, increasing fiscal constraints can pressure recreation staff to "market" their programs to meet the recreation needs of as many residents as possible. For all of these reasons, there is increased likelihood that recreation professionals, like other nursing home staff, will move in the direction of control.

To explore that likelihood, a study funded by the Professional Staff Congress of the City University of New York (PSC/CUNY), was conducted in 1985/86 at Lehman College, City University of New York. The purpose of the present paper is to report on the findings of that study which focused on staff and resident perceptions of positive and negative reinforcers on resident participation in nursing home recreation programs.

METHOD

This was a two-part study. One part addressed nursing home residents; the other, therapeutic recreation staff in nursing homes. One hundred fifty elderly from five nursing homes in the New York City metropolitan area participated in the first part of the study. These elderly were randomly selected from lists of residents who consented to participate in the study and who were judged by the recreation directors of their respective facilities as physically and mentally capable of responding to the questions. For the second part of the study, the sample was composed of all the therapeutic recreation staff at the five institutions represented in the resident sample, plus four other nursing homes in the area, for a total of 50 in the staff sample.

Variables for the questionnaires were drawn from items submitted by a panel of 10 certified therapeutic recreation professional in the New York area, all of whom had worked in nursing homes for at least 5 years. Panel members were not included in the study itself. Recurring items serves as the basis for the questions.

The client questionnaire was divided into four sections. The first sought demographic data. In the second, residents were asked to reflect on some of the activities which they regularly attended and then to agree or disagree (slightly, moderately, or strongly) with 35 stated reasons for attending. The third section asked their opinions about other residents' reasons for participating. In the fourth section, the residents were asked to reflect on activities in which they did not participate and, again, either to disagree or agree (slightly, moderately, or strongly) with reasons suggested for not participating.

The staff questionnaire was similar in structures. An introductory section gathered background information. Then there followed sections on staff opinions regarding reasons for resident participation in recreation activities and for their nonparticipation. The staff were also asked to rank-order 10 items which they perceived as rewards in their professional service and to indicate reinforcing methods which they might use to increase resident participation.

Graduate students from the Lehman College Recreation Program were trained to conduct the face-to-face interviews with the nursing home residents for the first part of the study. For the second part, where data were collected from the staff, written questionnaires were used. For all items, the following statistics were obtained: means, standard deviations, frequency distributions, and chi-squares.

FINDINGS

Part I–Resident Questionnaire

The average age for the group of 150 residents was 82 years; 42% (63) were males and 58% (87) were females. More than half the sample (56%) had 8 years of schooling or less, 34% had some high school, and the remaining 10% had attended college. More than half (54%) had been in the nursing home over 2 years. Mild to moderate visual impairments were reported by 68% of the participants, with mild to moderate hearing impairments indicated by 60% of the sample. While 38% were fully ambulatory, 34% were wheelchair-bound. The remainder required assistance for ambulation, using either a cane (12%) or a walker (16%).

Of the 35 items in which the residents were asked to reflect on the reasons for their recreation participation, the top 20% of the responses were ranked as follows:

Reason	Mean
The staff are kind and pleasant.	2.787
The activities are relaxing.	2.787
I like to socialize.	2.672
I want to keep active.	2.656
I find the activity interesting in itself.	2.574
It gives me a sense of accomplishment.	2.492
My daughter/son presses me to attend.	2.475

Although the two first-ranking responses were tied, the first shown, "the staff are kind and pleasant," had the highest score of "strongly agree"—86.9%. The response listed second, "the activity is relaxing," has a "strongly agree" score of 82.8%.

The lowest 20% of the responses were ranked as follows:

Reason	Mean
They serve refreshments.	0.795
The staff coax us to attend.	0.598

I like to compete for prizes.	0.566
I do what I am told.	0.270
We get special privileges for attending.	0.262
Staff pressure us to attend.	0.238
I am competing for a trophy.	0.197

Among the top seven chosen for participating, two might be seen as extrinsic motivators, namely, the kindness/pleasantness of the recreation staff and pressure from daughter/son. The other reasons all appear closer to the definition of intrinsic motivation. The lowest ranking choices are all examples of extrinsic motivation, with both positive and negative reinforcers represented.

In the third part of the questionnaire, residents strongly indicated that even if there were no prizes they would still attend their favored activities (mean, 2.918), and even if there were no refreshments they would still attend (mean, 2.083). They did entertain a moderate belief that other residents attended because of the refreshments, (mean, 2.024) and a less than moderate belief that others attended because of prizes (mean, 1.721) or in order to please the staff (mean, 1.664).

When it came to negative attribution, the following were the top-ranking choices for reasons for not participating in activities:

Reason	Mean
The activity in itself does not interest me.	1.484
Sometimes I like to be alone.	1.303
I find the activity tiring.	1.222
I have no talent/skill for the activity.	1.131
I have no experience at the activity.	1.066

Least frequently chosen reasons for not participating were these:

Reason	Mean
Too few residents attend.	0.377
The atmosphere/ambience is unpleasant.	0.287
I dislike the staff.	0.156
There are no prizes for the activity.	0.131
Refreshments are not served at the activity.	0.098

These very low means, all under 0.5, indicate close to total disagreement with the statements.

Part II–Staff Questionnaire

Among the 50 recreation staff members who participated in the study, ages ranged from 21 to 50 years, with a mean age of 31.9 years. Forty percent were male and 60% female. Of the 50, 10 were recreation directors, 12 were supervisors, 23 held the rank of recreation leader, and 5 were aides. Four percent had high school education. Twenty-six percent attended college, but did not have a degree, 46% had college degrees, and 24% had graduate degrees. One-half of the staff sample had worked in nursing home recreation for five years or more, 20% three to five years, and 30% one to three years.

Staff responses in general were not as strong as were those of the residents. For the section on attributing reasons for the residents' participation, the following were the most frequently chosen staff responses:

Reason	Mean
They find the activity relaxing.	2.538
They find the activity new and exciting.	2.231
They find the activity interesting in itself.	2.192
It gives them a sense of accomplishment.	2.192
It reminds them of past experiences.	2.077
It gives them a sense of belonging to a group.	2.038

Reasons for attending which were least frequently attributed to residents by staff:

Reason	Mean
The staff pressure them to attend.	1.154
They desire to please the staff.	1.154
They are competing for a trophy.	0.769
Their families pressure them to attend.	0.692
They want to avoid staff hostility.	0.462

Staff ranked residents' strongest reasons for not attending activities in the following way.

Reason	Mean
Depressive reaction to losses.	2.615
Diminished health status.	2.577
Inability to cope with changes in life-style.	2.423
Negative response to other participants.	2.192
No talent/skill for the activity.	2.038

Reasons for not attending which staff perceived as least likely to influence resident participation were:

Reason	Mean
Unpleasant atmosphere/ambience.	1.038
Negative response to changes in schedule.	1.038
Recreation setting inaccessible.	0.885
Resistance to staff coercion.	0.769
Unaware of activities.	0.692

In one section of the second questionnaire, staff were asked to rank 10 items in order of importance as rewards for their professional service. the overall mean responses (in descending order of choice) are:

Reward	Mean
Residents' declared satisfaction with the activities.	7.500
Functional improvement of residents.	6.922
Personal popularity among residents.	6.846
Consistently high numbers attending.	5.000
Decreased negative incidents among residents.	4.692
High ratings from government inspectors.	4.307
Special recognition from peers (recreation professionals).	4.269
Special recognition from administrator(s).	3.923
Approval of staff within the institution.	3.500
Approval of residents' families.	3.385

DISCUSSION OF FINDINGS

An arguable weakness of this study is, of course, the fact that it is based entirely on self-report. Notwithstanding this weakness, some points of interest can be noted. In proposing the attribution paradigm, Bem (1972) indicated that people make inferences about their motives for undertaking activities, attributing such motivation to extrinsic motivators when they perceive these to be controlling their behavior. When such reinforcers are not perceived, or if they seem to be ambiguous or insufficient, people tend to attribute the behavior to their own interests or desires. For nursing home residents, this may mean that when they can perceive no particular external reward for participating in recreation activities, they are likely to attribute such participation to personal preference or choice. Or it may suggest, in line with Skinner's theory mentioned earlier, that their reinforcers have been shifted to items which they find difficult to acknowledge. In this study, residents seem to be attributing their attendance largely to intrinsic motivators. Indeed, the more obvious extrinsic motivators, such as prizes, trophies, or refreshments, rank very low on the residents' list of reinforcers.

On the other hand, Iso-Ahola (1980) found that intrinsic motivation decreased as extrinsic rewards were supplied. His research was not carried out in a nursing home, however, and the central focus of the present study was on the reinforcers operating in nursing homes. Because so many usual reinforcers in peoples' lives are absolutely guaranteed in the nursing home, other unrecognized, contingent rewards assume great power to shape the residents' lives. This does not mean, of course, that everything in the nursing home becomes a reinforcer. It does suggest, however, that reinforcers in a nursing home may be quite different from what staff imagine.

For example, 86.9% of the residents in the study strongly agree that they attend activities because staff are kind and pleasant. This is the highest "strongly agree" rating of all items in both questionnaires. What does this suggest? Perhaps that the warmth of a personal relationship is a particularly powerful reinforcer in an institutional setting. This finding seems to fit with a similar, though not so strong, staff response. When asked to rank order 10 items as professionally rewarding, staff rated "Personal popularity among the residents" as the third highest. It would appear that the need to be liked or to be popular has very important stimulus value to both parties, but especially to the resident. This gives enormous power to recreation professionals in nursing homes. While one would not expect them to be unkind or unpleasant to clients, it is not unreasonable to suppose that the kindness and warmth might be increased or decreased as residents complied with therapeutic recreation expectations, cooperated with treatment goals, or otherwise behaved in accordance with staff norms.

The professional reward item ranked first by staff is "Residents' declared satisfaction with activities." This is surely not unexpected, given that a central feature of recreation is satisfaction. It takes on added importance in the light of the nursing home situation, where recreation is one of the very few services in which client satisfaction is of paramount importance. All of this contributes to the personal element and, perhaps, may strengthen its reinforcement potential even further.

Residents and staff agree on the importance of three positive motives for participation—feeling of relaxation accompanying the activity, finding the activity interesting in itself, and experiencing a sense of accomplishment through the activity. Both groups concur in selecting lack of talent as a reason for not participating in an activity and in seeing trophies as one of the weakest motives for participating. They disagree markedly about some of the other motivators. For example, residents see pressure from daughter or son as a very important reason for attending. Staff ranked this as one of the least important reinforcers.

On the whole, staff attributes nonattendance to items over which they (staff) have no control, for example, depression, diminished health status, inability to cope with changes in life-style, negative response to other participants, or lack of talent for the activity. On the other hand, nonattendance was least frequently attributed by staff to items over which they had some control, for example, unpleasant atmosphere, changes in schedule, inaccessible setting, resistance to staff coercion, or lack of awareness of activities. Staff seem inclined to follow a medical model of perception, that is, the influence of illness as a reason for not attending and the importance of functional improvement in residents as a reward for themselves (staff).

IMPLICATIONS

This study was undertaken as an exploratory search into the world of nursing home residents with the aim of clarifying some of the factors related to their participation in recreation programs. Despite the limiting effects of the subjective nature of the data gathered, the study does offer some suggestions for future research and for recreation policy and practice.

Further studies are needed comparing actual resident participation with various rewards. More data are required on staff's perceptions of the power of their warmth and kindness in shaping the resident's choices. Recreation professionals face a unique challenge in having to blend a clinical element with a human element in their service. The present study suggests that they are not aware of the kind of control they can exercise over their nursing home clients, who also represent a unique challenge because of their particular susceptibility to unexpected reinforcers.

In terms of policy and practice, a host of value questions confront recreation staff members because the heart of the leisure experience demands autonomy, whereas institutional life severely curtails and challenges autonomy. For example, whose value system will inform the completing of assessments, determine treatment goals and objectives, and guide the planning of recreation programs? How will the resident be protected from simply becoming the "subject" of the therapeutic recreation professional's plans for her or his behavior? What protection will she or he have from someone else's even well-intentioned manipulation? Will the resident share in the shaping of institutional and staff goals for her or his own care? Will she or he have veto power? How will conflicts between personal goals and institutional goals be resolved? What rights will the resident have to refuse treatment, if that treatment is a therapeutic recreation program? Does the staff have the right to move against the resident's wishes in the name of the resident's own good? If so, under what circumstances and with what process and protection for resident's rights?

What seems clear from the PSC/CUNY study is that therapeutic recreation professionals in nursing homes are either unaware of or reluctant to acknowledge their part in the intricately powerful control system operating within the institution. Training in behavior modification could help them recognize behavioral control and enable them to make informed choices about the use of such techniques. Such training would not only permit them to serve their clients in a more productive manner, but would also help to prevent the stress, burnout, and cynicism which may afflict professionals caught up in a powerful control system that they fail to recognize. Strengthened by such training, recreation professionals would be in a unique position to give leadership to other human service professionals in nursing homes by calling for a systematically articulated, controlled, and assessed use of behavior modification within the institution.

REFERENCES

Baltes, M., Burgess, & Stewart, R. (1980). Independence and dependence in self-care behaviors in nursing home residents: An operant-observational study. *International Journal of Behavioral Development, 3,* 489–500.

Bem, D. J. (1972). Self-perception theory. In L. Berkowitz, (ed.) *Advances in experimental social psychology.* New York: Academic Press.

Goffman, E. (1961). *Asylums.* Garden City, NY: Doubleday.

Halberg, K. J. & Howe-Murphy, R. (1985). The dilemma of an unresolved philosophy in therapeutic recreation. *Therapeutic Recreation Journal, 19* (3), 7–17.

Hunnicut, B. K. (1980). To cope in autonomy: Therapeutic recreation and the limits to professionalism and intervention. In *Expanding horizons in therapeutic recreation: Selected papers from the 1979 Midwest Symposium on Therapeutic Recreation.* Columbia, MO: University of Missouri Press.

Iso-Ahola, S. (Ed.). (1980). *Social psychological perspectives on leisure and recreation.* Springfield, IL: Charles C. Thomas.

Kraus, R. G. (1985). *Recreation program planning today.* Glenview, IL: Scott, Foresman & Co.

McDowell, C. F. (1986). Wellness and therapeutic recreation: challenges for service. *Therapeutic Recreation Journal, 20* (2), 27–38.

Mobily, K. E. (1985). A philosophical analysis of therapeutic recreation: What does it mean to say "We can be therapeutic?" Part I. *Therapeutic Recreation Journal, 18* (1), 14–27.

Peterson, C. A., & Gunn, S. L. (1984). *Therapeutic recreation program design: Principles and procedures.* Englewood Cliffs, NJ: Prentice-Hall.

Schmidt, M. G. (1982). Exchange and power in special settings for the aged. *International Journal of Aging and Human Development, 14* (3), 157–166.

Skinner, B. F. (1975). The ethics of helping people. *Criminal Law Bulletin 11,* 623–636.

Sylvester, C. D. (1985). The ethics of play, leisure and recreation in the twentieth century. *Abstracts: 1985 Symposium on Leisure Research.* Alexandria, VA: National Recreation and Parks Association.

8

THE DEVELOPMENT OF AGE-APPROPRIATE OUTDOOR PLAYGROUND BEHAVIORS IN SEVERELY DISABLED CHILDREN

Michael E. Crawford

The purpose of this investigation was to provide a direct test of recreational programming by the theory of Least Restricted Environment (LRE) within a community-based setting. This study developed and tested techniques for teaching age-appropriate, outdoor playground skills to severely disabled children (N=5). Multiple baseline behavioral experiments were developed within an ABAB reversal design for each participant. The results indicated significant increases in high quality leisure behavior for the majority of participants. However, natural environmental complexity and off-task participant behaviors contributed to nonresults for several participants. This study tested the applicability of contemporary educational theories and behavioral techniques when applied within a normal community based recreational environment. Further development of skill-acquisition techniques and maintenance and generalization procedures is needed if the severely disabled are to be effectively served in nonsegregated recreational environments according to LRE doctrine.

Leisure skill training is important to the habilitation and community integration of severely handicapped individuals. Most of those individuals have ample discretionary time, but usually do not use their leisure in constructive ways (Wehman & Schleien,

1981). Typically, inappropriate social behaviors, such as hand flapping, body rocking, self-abuse, and bizarre verbalizations are exhibited. Those behaviors may lead to reinstitutionalization or reduce the likelihood of integration into the community. Within the last few years human service professionals have attempted to provide service to disabled individuals in community and non-institutional settings according to the Least Restrictive Environment (LRE) doctrine. According to LRE, only those skills or activities which have the potential of being performed in the presence of, or in interaction with, nondisabled peers should be selected for instruction. Programming that does not include the LRE philosophy could result in the acquisition of leisure skills that meet the substandard performance demands of protective segregated settings.

There have been relatively few studies evaluating the acquisition of age-appropriate leisure skills in severely handicapped participants within community settings. Early studies focused on developing leisure skills in moderately retarded adults and adolescents (Johnson & Bailey, 1977; Matson & Marchetti, 1977; Schleien, Kiernan, & Wehman, 1981a). Those studies included such leisure behaviors as playing table games, throwing darts, acquiring physical fitness skills, and operating a stereo and were mainly conducted in group homes. More recently the majority of leisure skill research has studied moderately retarded children (Certo, Scheien, & Hunter, 1983; Bishop & French, 1983) and severely retarded adults (Stainback, Stainback, Wehman, & Spaugiers, 1983). Regardless of these limited successes, researchers note that the process of applying educational technology to severely multihandicapped participants in normalized community settings remains largely unexplored (Baumgart, Brown, Pumpian, Nisket, Ford, Sweet, Messina, & Schroeder, Hammer, 1984).

There has been, and continues to be, a paucity of research in playground assessment even with normal able-bodied youngsters (Polgar, 1976; Beckwith, 1977; Rutherford, 1979; Parnell & Ketterson, 1980). The research with special populations is more attentuate (Carter, 1978; Carlson, 1979; Strickland, 1979; Crawford, 1983). Much of the underdevelopment of this literature is due to the need for adequate assessment instrumentation and the lack of a comprehensive theory of play engagement for the playground (Gabbard & LeBlanc, 1980).

Though an abundance of materials exists on the subject of outdoor play environments, little of this material addresses specific procedures for conducting outdoor play programs for the disabled. Most designers and manufacturers of playground equipment address the programming issue through vague statements about growth and development. They include in their descriptions of outdoor play equipment statements such as "unlocking developmental potentials" and "magically sparking the young mind's imagination" (Crawford, 1979). They hypothesize that repeated opportunities or exposure to playgrounds will somehow lead to spontanous participation behaviors.

While it is true that normal preschool populations have demonstrated spontaneous and original movement behaviors when introduced to novel play experiences (Polgar, 1976), no such evidence exists for their more severely afflicted mentally retarded and physically disabled peers. Thus, a more systematic programming approach is suggested, one which would encourage and guide outdoor play experiences through the development and validation of specific instructional procedures relevant to community-based settings.

PURPOSE

Educational experts agree that for most every type and combination of handicapping condition a productive educational strategy has been developed and validated in a research setting. Unfortunately, what researchers know has not been systematized as methodology for recreational programmers to use in natural community settings. What is needed is an effective demonstration of the relevance and applicability of systematic instruction for the multihandicapped in community settings. Once such techniques are field-tested and validated, the rationale for programming in normalized environments will no longer rest solely on the philosophical argument of the LRE doctrine.

The purpose of this study was to directly test the applicability of LRE theory. The paucity of research that supports field-demonstrated effectiveness of the LRE theory serves as a barrier to further development and implementation of this concept. By selecting a specific recreational environment (outdoor playgrounds) and population (severely disabled children), this study was able to identify factors important to implementing LRE theory. Additionally, target areas for continued development and refinement became apparent. Finally, this study provided further validation of the precision teaching techniques reported as successful in previous LRE work (Stainback et al, 1983) by providing yet another forum and test of their instructional power. Through the development and validation of playground training procedures it was hoped that the goal of LRE programming could be realized in yet another important recreational setting previously unsubstantiated by applied behavioral research.

METHODOLOGY

Subjects

The subjects of this study were multihandicapped children aged 7–12 ($N=5$) who resided at the same community-based group home. According to the American Association on Mental Deficiency Standards, all were in the severe range of mental retardation both intellectually and adaptively (Nihiria, Foster, Shelhaas, and Leland, 1975). Each had experienced multiple living and school placements. Several had acute episodes of self-aggression and aggression directed toward others. While all were ambulatory, some possessed additional sensory (sight, hearing, tactile) and physical (spina bifida, cerebral palsy, multiple sclerosis) impairments which required assistive devicing and appliances (catheter, Milwaukee brace, Canadian crutches, extreme magnificantion glasses, etc.). Further elaboration of specific subject characteristics occurs in the case-study results section of this report.

Setting

All phases of the study took place on a playground located within a large public park. The playground equipment was of traditional design (i.e., no rocketship slides or abstract wooden structures, etc.) and included merry-go-round, high slide, dome climber, swing set, rocking horses, climbing poles, teeter-totters, and stepping stumps. No attempt was made to control for antecedent social or environmental factors which surrounded the immediate playground area as those stimuli were part of the experimental design of the study. Possible antecedent distractors included a jogging trail with exercise stations, a large picnic area, a golf course with motorized carts, a soccer field, and an access road with pedestrian and vehicular traffic. The intensity of antecedent conditions varied dramatically from day to day with weekends predictably exerting a greater potential for distraction on participant performances.

Data Collection and Training Procedures

This study employed an ABAB reversal design. Each of the four subphases is described in detail below.

Sub-I (Baseline). Systematic observations were made of the particpants' behaviors on the playground during unstructured free play. This subphase lasted for 5 days and served as a pre-intervention baseline for behavior patterns and competencies. Two trained observers were present at each session. A momentary time-sampling technique using 30-second intervals was employed to record the quality of leisure behavior of the participants. The three categories of behavior which were operationally defined and coded during the baseline process were the same as those defined by Schleien et al. (1981b). They consisted of (a) high quality leisure behavior (HQ), (b) low quality leisure behavior (LQ), and (c) inappropriate social behavior (I). The selection and frequency of interaction with playground equipment were also recorded to determine which apparatus held intrinsic motivational value.

Sub-II (Instruction/Reinforcement). Following analysis of baseline levels, leisure skill instruction was begun for each subject. Any playground apparatus during baseline that had elicited either (a) partial high quality leisure behaviors (i.e., attempted to climb ladder on slide or sat on swing and rocked) and/or (b) low quality behavior of a sustained or frequent nature (i.e., returned to gaze at other children on merry-go-round, handled chains on swings, etc.) were hypothesized to be more intrinsically reinforcing than playground apparatus which were ignored. Thus each appropriate playground apparatus (according to the criteria stated above) and a related playground skill were included in a multiple baseline training paradigm for each subject. This method of selecting target behaviors resulted in as few as one and as many as four different training programs per subject.

A complete task-analysis was conducted for each playground apparatus and behavior. Behaviors were either forward or backward chained in constructing the training hierarchies. The completed task analysis ranged from 12 to 33 steps depending upon the skill involved. An example of a complete task-analysis may be found in Table 1. Participants received one-to-one individual training sessions 4 days per week for 1-hour time periods. Training days and times were randomly selected at the beginning of each training week with some artificial restrictions for school days and the group home meal schedules. Each day the order of training for the various leisure skills was randomly determined. Participants received leisure skill instruction for each designated skill twice within each instructional hour. At the end of every individual instruction session, the participant involved was tested. Data collection involved marking whether a training step was performed independently by the participant when provided a verbal cue and model. Data were collected on two trials for each active training step.

Training was conducted by second-year graduate students in a therapeutic recreation master's program. All 4 trainers had at least 1 year of full-time clinical experience with clients of similar abilities and in parallel training situations. A full day of training was conducted with each trainer, complete with field trials, using equipment and training procedures with clients of similar ability not directly involved in the study. All task-analyses were developed by the primary investigator and by a therapist with a master's degree in special education and 6 years of postdegreee experience. The training procedures used represented a slight modification of those employed by Stainback et al. (1983) in work with severe and profoundly retarded subjects.

Instructors used an instructional cue hierarchy system (Alberto & Schofield, 1979) in which the instructor first waits for an independent response (subject self-initiates and completes the step). If the response is not emitted, the participant is provided the level(s) of assistance necessary to elicit the response. More specifically, if the participant did not perform the step after verbal cue (e.g., place your foot on the ladder) and model were presented, the instructor (a) prompted by gesturing and/or touching the body part to be moved on the participant and, if necessary, (b) physi-

TABLE 1
Task Analysis for Swinging

1. The participant will approach the equipment without exhibiting a fear or flight response.
2. The participant will select a swing to use by pointing to a free swing.
3. The participant will approach the swing by walking up to it in a straight line, successfully avoiding the arc of other swings in the area.
4. The participant will successfully mount the swing by turning and sitting without losing balance.
5. The participant will sit passively on the swing while maintaining balance.
6. The participant will hold the chains (ropes) one in each hand at shoulder height.
7. The participant will allow a back-and-forth motion initiated by an adult helper.
8. The participant will lean back in the swing while simultaneously extending the legs and pulling back on the chains.
9. The participant will lean forward in the swing while simultaneously flexing the legs and pushing forward on the chains.
10. The participant will repeat steps 8 and 9 in sequence in a successful "pumping" motion for at least a 30-second performance.
11. The participant will drag the feet in a breaking motion until the swing has stopped moving.
12. The participant will successfuly dismount from the swing without losing balance.
13. The participant will walk forward 5 steps successfully clearing the arc of other swings before turning to walk away.

cally guided the participant through the step. Modeling was provided concurrently with the verbal cue as the initial step because most playground settings would have normal models engaged in similar behaviors as an antecendent to participation. Reinforcement was provided for movement or progress toward the desired behavior. Reinforcement procedures varied per participant with regard to the type and schedule of reinforcement used. In several instances it was necessary to work with primary reinforcers (e.g., fruit juice or M and M candies) in order to maintain instructional control. Other participants were able to stay on task by simply using continuous social and physical prompts and consequences. However, all participants were shaped away from continuous primary reinforcers and toward intermittent social reinforcers (e.g., smile, head nod, verbal praise, and/or parallel participation). Participants were considered to have reached criterion when for 2 consecutive days she or he consistently and appropriately responded to the verbal cue and model for 90 percent of the steps of a complete task-analysis. When mastery was achieved for one particular step of the task-analysis, this step was deleted from training, and further training focused on another step within the task-analysis until all steps were mastered.

Sub-III (Return to Baseline). Following a sufficient period of trials in which participants reached criterion for at least one new playground leisure skill, a return to baseline was implemented. Daily excursions to the playground continued during this time, but no instruction/reinforcement took place. Data collection was carried out in the same manner as during instructional sessions. Data collection and trainers unfamiliar to participants collected data during this phase eliminating incidental reinforcement elements associated with the regular personnel.

Sub-IV (Instruction/Reinforcement Reinstated). During the final subphase, program instruction and reinforcement were reinstated until behaviors for newly acquired playground leisure skills returned to criterion levels and were maintained for at least 5 days.

Interrater Reliability

Interrater reliability measures were taken during each day of playground training. At least two reliability checks occurred on a weekly basis for each apparatus training program per subject. Reliability coefficients were computed using the formula: agreements divided by agreements plus disagreements times 100. Agreement occurred when both observers marked either a yes or no when a step in the task-analysis was performed by a participant. Interrater reliability coefficients ranged from 93% to 100%, with a mean of 96%. Observers positioned themselves in unobtrusive locations and shielded checklists with magazine covers.

RESULTS

During baseline observations of particpants none displayed preintervention high quality playground behaviors. Case presentations which provide elaboration of both success and nonresult information attained for each participant follow:

Case 1—John. At age 7, John was the youngest of this study's participants. In addition to severe retardation, John possessed ataxic cerebral palsy. John's behavior was cyclical. He changed from quiet, imitative, and smiling behaviors to scolding others, often scowling and shaking his finger. Despite his moodiness, he was not aggressive. He would allow hands-on manipulation for only a few moments. At times he displayed rocking and pacing behaviors.

During baseline John spent the majority of his time (70% of intervals observed) with two playground apparatuses. Use of both of these (swings and rocking horses) were selected as target behaviors for John. During initial instruction and reinforcement John displayed steady improvement with the rocking horse and after 36 instructional sessions could mount, balance, and hold on while rocking the horse back and forth at least 3 times. Similar behaviors for the swing were not achieved. John was unable to learn the subskill for "pumping" the swing (extending the legs while simultaneously using the hands to pull back on the chains) and would protest by dismounting when trainers attempted co-active assistance. Training for the swing was discontinued after 27 sessions when after 5 consecutive days John refused to let trainers assist him in any way.

When reinforcement and instruction were terminated during the reversal phase, John's new rocking horse skill quickly decelerated. Several days of incomplete performances were followed by 3 consecutive days of zero interaction with the equipment. During this time John often gazed in the direction of the golf course and appeared to track the movements of the motorized carts whenever one was near. When instructions and reinforcement were reinstated (subphase four) John regained criterion for the rocking horse skill after just 2 days. This level of participation was maintained for 10 days.

Case 2—Billy. Billy was 11 years old and in addition to severe retardation was afflicted by spina bifida. He wore a Milwaukee brace and a catheter. Despite the brace and spinal condition Billy's ambulation, though slow and shufflelike, was generally good. Billy had impulse-control difficulties and would frequently place his hands to his face, one by his ear and the other over his mouth, while uttering a high pitched scream. At times Billy would self-abuse by biting his hands and wrists. These episodes were often triggered by trainer demands for performance. Billy's physical condition prevented him from participating in certain playground activities. High aerial stunts (e.g., dome climber and high slide) were not possible, and acitivities with impact potential (e.g., bumping the ground while seated on the teeter-totter) were also exlcuded on physician's orders.

During baseline Billy initiated almost no interaction with playground equipment (only 12% of intervals observed). However 60% of the interactions noted involved the swings. A single target behavior for swings was established for subphase two: instruction and reinforcement. After 47 sessions, training attempts were discontinued. Over the course of training Billy became increasingly self-stimulatory and self-abusive. Training staff were never able to gain instructional control long enough to make a difference in the quality of playground performances.

Case 3—Jane. At age 12, Jane's severe retardation was complicated by a recent diagnosis of childhood multiple sclerosis. She would frequently fall when running and often injured her knee while doing so (scrapes and cuts). She wore extreme magnification glasses.

During baseline Jane was the most active of all participants initiating equipment-directed behaviors for 80% of all intervals observed. Four playground target behaviors were established for Jane which included use of teeter-totter, dome climber, high slide, and merry-go-round.

Training was discontinued for the dome climber and high slide after 16 and 21 sessions, respectively. Once Jane achieved the climbing and grip skills necessary to reach a position of height on the equipment, both Jane and the training staff discovered she had a real fear of height. After several days of "kitten-up-a-tree" behaviors, during which Jane would tantrum and refuse to move until staff carried her down from the equipment, training was terminated.

Jane did achieve criterion for both mounting, maintaining grip and balance, riding, and dismounting the teeter-totter and merry-go-round apparatus after 41 and 59 sessions, respectively. During the reversal phase skill levels declined to below 50% of stated criteria for both apparatus after just 2 days. However, after reinforcement and instruction were reinstated in subphase four, skills returned to criterion levels for the teeter-totter (5 days) and merry-go-round (3 days) relatively quickly. These behaviors were successfully maintained for 10 days.

Case 4—Mark. Mark's borderline severe/profound retardation was complicated by ataxic cerebral palsy. Additionally, occupational and physical therapists believed Mark to be tactile defensive. At 10 years of age he still had difficulty with consistent and appropriate toilet behaviors. Mark displayed many bizarre behaviors. He would sit for long periods of time while blowing air through his lips making a buzzing noise and simultaneously flipping his left hand and fingers up and down across his mouth. Acute episodes of aggression against peers and staff were displayed in the form of pinches and slaps delivered to the top of hands and forearms. Also, occasional outbursts of self-abuse, mainly in the form of slapping the tops of this thighs with his open hands, occurred.

During baseline Mark spent approximately 35% of observed intervals interacting with playground equipment. Two apparatuses, the merry-go-round and swings, accounted for 90% of the interactions. Use of both apparatus became target behaviors. After 38 sessions, when Mark's abuse toward others and himself dominated training for 4 consecutive days, training for both was discontinued.

Case 5—Lisa. Lisa was 12 years old, severely retarded, and afflicted with spina bifida. Her gait, although assisted by Canadian crutches, was smooth and controlled. She actively sought staff attention and would become aggressive toward peers if interactions between herself and staff were complicated by a peer's presence. Her interactions with adults were often attention-seeking behaviors, such as poking, tickling, and teasing.

During baseline observation Lisa spent over 50% of her time engaging playground equipment. Two apparatuses, the swings and rocking horses, received 65% and 28% of her attention, respectively, resulting in both being selected for target behavior training. During subphase two training, Lisa achieved criterion for the swing after 51 sessions. A great proportion of sessions focused on the subskill of using the arms and legs in tandem to move the swing (23 of 51 sessions devoted to learning to "pump") and in dragging the feet to stop the swing (13 of 51 sessions).

Lisa was unable to reach criterion for the rocking horse skill (training discontinued after 27 sessions). She was unable to move the rocking horse back and forth and maintain independent balance. Instructors hypothesized that the tension on the base spring resulted in too strong and fast a tempo in the rocking motion for Lisa to anticipate and control (as opposed to the very steady, smooth, and predictable motion of the swing). Lisa's new playground skills were successfully maintained at the criterion level for 8 of the next 10 sessions.

Analysis of Group Trends

For all participants, baseline data at the playground indicated that repeated exposure without intervening training did not result in acquisition of skills. A pattern of steady improvement was evident during reinforcement and instruction (subphase II) for the 3 participants who achieved new playground skills. Between 36 and 59 training sessions were required for new playground behaviors to reach criterion levels of performance. Unfortunately skills obtained during reinforcement and instruction training were not maintained once intervention strategies were removed during the reversal phase. These skills returned rapidly however once instruction and reinforcement procedures were reinstated, and behaviors were successfully maintained for up to 10 days afterwards.

Although the playground training focused on specific leisure target behaviors, the effects of training were not restricted to those discrete responses. Trainers and related direct-care and educational staff noted that overall evaluations of social skills (improved attention to task, deceleration of self-stimulatory behaviors, etc.) improved for those participants who learned new leisure skills over the course of training. This apparent multiplier effect of training was unanticipated and formal measures were not employed to samples rates of these behaviors pre- and postintervention. It is reported as a finding of this study based on the consensus of those trained participating observers who had extensive knowledge of the participants behavior patterns.

Unfortunately, not all participants acquired new playground behaviors. In fact, even those participants who learned new skills failed to reach similar levels of ability for other target behaviors. In several instances it was necessary to discontinue training.

Frequently recorded behaviors which prevented trainers from achieving and maintaining instructional control included:

Performance (unnecessary movements): (a) aborted or abbreviated attempts to mounting; (b) grasped and clung to trainers for support; (c) swung arms over head and displayed other extraneous movements.

Tempo (noncontinuous, stopping, or retreating behaviors): (a) refused to perform once in place; (b) soiled clothing through urination to protest delay in dismount (e.g., time needed to stop merry-go-round or get down from climber, etc.); (c) engaged in self-abuse to protest delay in dismount or show displeasure with mount (e.g., biting, scratching, slapping, etc.); (d) abused others (scratching, biting, etc.); (e) shook head "no" or said "no"; (f) screamed or emitted unpleasant verbal sounds.

Attending Behaviors (looking away, unnecessary focus on equipment or self): (a) began disruptive behavior after very short duration on equipment; (b) threw tantrum or cried while pointing to another area of the playground; (c) looked away from adult assistant when asked a question; (d) repeated requests to ride in a golf cart or similary focused on other environmental antecedent conditions.

A number of positive participation behaviors for participants were noted regardless of skill level. Those included: (a) smiled frequently; (b) emitted pleasant verbalizations; (c) clapped hands; (d) waved arms above head; (e) said the words "good" or "I'm happy," etc.; (f) protested at having to dismount equipment to give another user a turn; (g) protested at having to leave playground to return home.

DISCUSSION

Despite a careful application of currently recommended training procedures (Stainback et al., 1983 and Baumgart et al.; 1982), certain combinations of environmental complexity and negative participant behaviors overwhelmed the instructional procedure, and learning decelerated for several participants. Others were relatively successful in acquiring new age-appropriate playground behaviors.

The mixed results of the study are disappointing and make precise interpretation difficult. However, several general implications which might prove valuable for future investigations warrant highlighting.

The first implication is that at least some severely disabled individuals can learn high-quality leisure skills in normalized environments when provided systematic instruction. This supports the findings of a variety of contemporary researchers (Stainback, et al., 1983; Schleien et al., 1981b; Horst, Wehman Hill, Bailey, 1980; Adkins & Matson, 1980). The number of training sessions required for participants to achieve criterion varied dramatically. Such variance can be attributed to several factors. First, the abilities and learning rates of participants were considerably different; and second, task difficulty and the number of steps and branch discriminations across the task-analyses of the various playground behaviors were not uniform.

The second clear implication involves the question of long-term maintenance of leisure skills. The duration of behavioral improvements obtained without continued programmatic support is questionable, given the rapid declines observed during the reversal phases of this study. Although behaviors were maintained on a limited basis once programmatic assistance was reinstated, the data suggests regular use of skills is essential for maintenance.

For those participants in which acquisition of primary target behaviors were successful, the effects of leisure skill training appeared to carry over to social behaviors on which training did not specifically focus (i.e., observations of increases in appropriate motor and social skills). Because of the lack of specific pre- and postmeasurements of the observations and attitudes of parents, direct-care staff, and teachers, it is difficult to elaborate on what this apparent multiplier effect means. Future studies should incorporate specific controls for antecedent and consequential social parameters.

Future research should examine the extension of leisure behaviors to multiple normalized settings. The generalization goal is one which most contemporary authorities in recreation and rehabilitation recognize as essential to successful living in integrated community environments (Voeltz, Wuerch, & Wilcox, 1982; Wehman & Schleien, 1981). What effects do different playground and varied environmental antecedent conditions have on performance?

A larger issue is raised by the results of the study. Will it be possible to train, generalize, and maintain high quality leisure skills in multiple domains of funtioning across multiple natural environments for a single severely handicapped individual? How elaborate and extensive can the leisure skill repertoire for such an individual become, and what levels of personal and programmatic assistance will be required to develop and maintain such potentials once discovered?

This study identified the structuring of the outdoor play environment through a carefully developed and presented training program, as a necessary prerequisite for the development of improved leisure behaviors. However, the results also demonstrated that successful LRE programming for some severely disabled children is still a tenuous proposition. The present results offer only limited promise and suggest that procedures for training high quality leisure skill in normalized settings need significant improvement.

REFERENCES

Adkins, J. & Matson, J. L. (1980). Teaching institutionalized mentally retarded adults socially appropriate leisure skills. *Mental Retardation, 18;* 249–252.

Alberto, P., & Schofield, P. L. (1979). An instructional interaction pattern for the severly handipcapped. *Teaching Exceptional Children, 12,* 16–19.

Auxter, D. (1983). Generalization of motor skills from training to natural environments. *Journal of Applied Behavioral Analysis, 21,* 237–242.

Baumgart, D., Brown, L., Pumpian, I., Nishet, J., Ford, A., Sweet M., Messina, R., & Schroeder, J. (1982). Principle of partial participation and individualized adaptions in educational programs for severly handicapped students. *TASH Journal, 7,* 17–26.

Beckwith, J. (1977). Play equipment structures. A private publication disseminated at the 1977 National AAHPERD Convention, Kansas City, Kansas.

Bishop, P. & French, R. (1983). Effects of reinforcers on attending behavior of

severly handicapped boys in physical education. *Journal for Special Educators, 18*(4), 49–57.
Carlson, L. (1979). An interdisciplinary approach to the design of play environments for severely profoundly retarded institutional residents. Paper presented at the Annual International Convention, The Council for Exceptional Children, Dallas, Texas, Session F–76.
Carter, A. (1978). Barrier-free playground: A playground for all children. *Progressive Architecture, 59*(4), 90–91.
Certo, N., Scheien, S., & Hunter, D. (1983). An ecological assessment inventory to facilitate community recreation participation by severely disabled individuals. *Therapeutic Recreation Journal, 17*(3), 29–38.
Crawford, M. E. (1979). Therapeutic recreation service and creative playgrounds. *Nebraska Journal of Health, Physical Education, and Recreation, 1*, 16–19.
Crawford, M. E. (1983). Development of a playground movement inventory. Doctoral dissertation, Indiana University, Bloomington. University of Oregon Microform Publications BF723.M6.
Gabbard, C. P., & LeBlanc, E. (1980). Movement activity levels on traditional and contemporary playground structures. *ERIC/EDRS* # 198 082.
Hammer, E. (1984). Process teaching: A systems approach to the education of multi-handicapped deaf-blind children. Paper presented at Collier Center for Communication Disorder Workshop, Dallas, TX. Grant #OEG–0–74–7930–06.
Horst, G., Wehman, P. Hill, J. W., & Bailey, C. (1980). Developing chronologically age-appropriate leisure skills in severely multi-handicapped adolescents: Three case studies. In P. Wehman & J. W. Hill (Eds.), *Instructional programming for severely handicapped youth: A community integration approach*, Richmond: Virginia Commonwealth University School of Education.
Johnson, M., & Bailey J. (1977). The modification of leisure behavior in a halfway house for retarded women. *Journal of Applied Behavioral Analysis, 10*, 349–367.
Matson, J. L., & Marchetti, A. (1977). A comparison of leisure skills training procedures for the mentally retarded. *Journal of Applied Behavior Analysis, 10*, 349–367.
Nihiria, K., Foster, R., Shelhaas, M., Leland, H. (1975). *AAMD Adaptive Behavior Scale* (Revision). Washington, DC: American Association on Mental Deficiency.
Parnell, K. & Ketterson, P. (1980). What should a playground offer? *The Elementary School Journal, 80*(5), 233–239.
Polgar, S. K. (1976). The social context of games: Or when is play not play? *Socialogy of Education, 49*, 265–271.
Rutherford, G. W. (1979). HIA hazard analysis: Injuries associated with public playground equipment. U.S. Consumer Product Safety Commission.
Schleien, S., Wehman, P., & Kiernan, J. (1981a). Teaching leisure skills to severely handicapped adults: And age-appropriate darts game. *Education and training of the mentally retarded, 16*, 13–19.
Schleien, S., Kiernan, J., & Wehman, P. (1981b). Evaluation of an age appropriate leisure skills program for moderately retarded adults. *Education and Training of the Mentally Retarded. 16*, 13–19.
Stainback, S., Stainback, W., Wehman, P., & Spangiers, L. (1983). Acquisition and generalization of physical fitness exercises in three profoundly retarded adults. *TASH Journal, 8*, 46–55.
Strickland, E. (1979). Selected free play research: Implications for MH/MR children. Paper presented at the Annual International Convention, The Council

for Exceptional Children, Dallas, TX, Session F–76.

Voeltz, L. M., Wuerch, B. B., & Wilcox, B. (1982). Leisure/recreation: Preparation for independence, integration and self fulfillment. In B. Wilcox & G.T. Bellamy, *Design of high school programs for severely handicapped students*. Baltimore: Paul H. Brooks Publishing Co.

Wehman, P., & Schleien, S. (1981) *Leisure programs for handicapped persons: Adaptions, techniques and curriculum.* Baltimore: University Park Press.

9

A COMPARISON OF RELAXATION THERAPY AND PHYSICAL ACTIVITY IN DECREASING HYPERACTIVITY IN THE MENTALLY RETARDED

Paul Heitzenrater
Francis A. McGuire
Robert W. McLellan
Gordon E. Howard

The study was undertaken to determine if relaxation therapy and physical activity are effective in calming hyperactive, mentally retarded individuals. Thirty hyperactive, mentally retarded subjects ranging in age from 12 to 20 were selected from structured classroom settings based on past hyperactive behavior. The subjects were first monitored using the Doubros and Daniels (1966) hyperactivity checklist. This rates subjects according to the number of hyperactive responses made during a 30-minute time period. Subjects were then randomly assigned to a relaxation therapy, physical therapy, or a control group. After each treatment, the subjects were again monitored for the number of hyperactive behaviors exhibited. Results indicated relaxation therapy was most effective in reducing hyperactivity. Relaxation therapy may thus be part of a program professionals can utilize to decrease hyperactive behavior by the mentally retarded.

Hyperactivity in both normal and mentally retarded populatations is a major concern. Although characteristics of a hyperactive child are easily recognized, Lahey, Stempnick, Robinson, and Tyroler (1978) point out that there are definitional problems surrounding the term which cannot be resolved until dimensions of behavior can be identified and related to hyperactivity in some way. Firestone, Peters, River, and Knights (1978) described hyperactivity as behaviors shown by a heterogeneous group of children, including overactivity, irritability, impulsivity, and attention deficits. Hyperactivity is characteristic of some mentally retarded persons and is evidenced by a child moving continuously from one activity to another, being easily distracted and excited, and displaying high levels of motor activity (Doubros & Daniels, 1966; Wade, 1973). It is commonly believed that overactivity is one personality trait of mentally retarded persons, especially those with central nervous system defects (Doubros & Daniels, 1966).

Several types of therapy have been used for treatment of hyperactive, mentally retarded persons. These have included drug therapy, behavior modification, and some relaxation therapy (Doubros & Daniels, 1966; Wade, 1973; O'Leary, Pelham, Rosenbaum, & Price, 1976; Goetyl, Granbers, & Berkowitz, 1977; Harvey, 1979). Drugs, particularly lithium, are commonly used in controlling activity levels and aggression in mentally retarded people (O'Leary et al., 1976; Goetyl et al., 1977). Stimulant therapy is effective with many (50–70%) hyperactive children, but some do not respond (Goetyl et al., 1977). Medication alone does not always return children to normal functioning and drug intervention cannot always be used when hyperactivity occurs at the child's home (O'Leary et al., 1976).

Alternatives to drug therapy and the resulting dependency on drugs are becoming increasingly popular. Behavior modification is common with the hyperactive. Ayllon, Layman, and Kandel (1975) found that a behavior modification program controlled hyperactivity at a level comparable to that of drug therapy. At the same time, subjects' academic performance improved 12%. Some consider adult attention towards the child as an effective reinforcer (Allen, Henke, Harris, Baer, & Reynolds, 1967; Cunningham & Barkley, 1979; Mash & Johnston, 1982). Doubros and Daniels (1966) tested hyperactive boys in a differential reinforcement procedure and found that treatment with reinforcers lowered frequency of the undesirable behavior and reduced variability of the hyperactive output.

Physical activities have also proven to be a method of releasing energy and aggression in the mentally retarded (Berkson & Davenport, 1962; Flavell, 1973). Play can act to decrease or eliminate inappropriate social behavior, violent outbursts, and aggression, as well as inhibit stereotypic rocking, bizarre vocal sounds, and self-inflicted aggression that are typical of severely and profoundly retarded individuals (Paloutzian, Hasazi, Streifel, & Edgar, 1971; Wade, 1973; Morris & Dolker, 1974).

Relaxation therapy is a recent method in dealing with hyperactive, mentally retarded persons. It has the potential to become an alternative to conventional methods of therapy. Relaxation training was tested by Harvey (1979) and found to be helpful in facilitating group and individual psychotherapy, eliminating specific phobias, reducing general anxiety and behavior difficulties, and coping with academic problems. Harvey used the mentally retarded as his subjects. Day and Sadek (1982) treated children in war-zone areas with relaxation therapy and found subjects had a lower anxiety level and were calmer than a control group. Rickard, Thrasher, and Elkins (1984) have examined responses of mentally retarded persons to relaxation instruction. Relaxation therapy and physical activity may be alternatives to drug therapy and behavior modification methods.

The purpose of the study was to determine if relaxation therapy or physical activity was effective in calming hyperactive, mentally retarded individuals. The hypothesis of this research was that relaxation techniques would be equally effective as physical activities in reducing hyperactive behaviors in the mentally retarded.

METHOD

Subjects

The subjects used for this study were from a large state institution and training center for the mentally retarded in Colorado. Thirty mentally retarded subjects were initially selected from structured activity classroom settings because of their past hyperactive behavior. They were later randomly placed in one of three groups. The subjects ranged in age between 12 and 20 and included 12 females and 18 males.

Evaluation

The subjects were monitored using the Doubros and Daniels (1966) checklist of hyperactivity. This checklist was based on behaviors shown frequently by hyperactive subjects. The hyperactive behaviors recorded are categorized into four types: locomotive body movements (i.e., walking, crawling, climbing on fixtures, picking up unassigned toys, etc.), stationary body movements (i.e., shuffling feet, scratching, mouthing objects, etc.), destructive behavior (i.e., kicking, throwing away toys or materials, pounding toys, etc.), and communication (i.e., talking constantly, shouting, whistling, etc.). Doubros and Daniels (1966), in testing the instrument, compared both interobserver and inter-item correlation based on 8 observation days. They reported a Spearman's rank-difference index of 1.0 indicating observers rated subjects in the same way with respect to total frequency of hyperactive responses. Item to item analysis indicated individual observer correlations ranging from .83 to .98 across the items on the checklist.

In this study the subjects were observed in groups of 10 by 5 observers. These observers were individuals with whom the subjects were familiar so that a relatively normal environment would be present. Each observer was randomly given 2 subjects to observe for 30 minutes. Due to previously reported reliability and apparent ease of use of the checklist, no interrater crosschecks were effected. Monitoring was done on a time-sampling method of observation. This was the procedure utilized by Doubros and Daniels (1966). The observers monitored the three groups before treatment and the same groups after the treatment, but were blind to the treatment given. There is the possibility observers may have determined which group the subjects were in, yet the objectivity of the instrument should have eliminated bias. After all the subjects had been observed, they were randomly placed in three treatment groups (10 per group). According to Wade (1973), group size among the mentally retarded has no significant effect when testing hyperactive behavior. One group was taken to a darkened, quiet area and told to lie down on mats. Music that was relaxing and soft was used to calm the individuals while they closed their eyes, kept quiet, and relaxed muscle groups as the leader went around touching these muscle groups. Whereas relaxation therapy proponents sometimes suggest that touching be avoided, our procedure allowed for closing of the eyes and a darkened room, while keeping the subjects awake. It was felt that touching would be less of a stimulus to the subjects than seeing movement by leaders or other subjects. The music included harp, keyboards, and flute taken from Halpern's (1978) antifrantic collection. This type of progressive muscle relaxation technique has been used to calm disruptive, autistic adolescents (Marholin, 1979). The relaxation group was treated 4 times, 2 times a day for approximately 45 minutes each period. It has been found that relaxation therapy is more effective if given more than once daily, (Harvey, 1979; Marholin, 1979). Posttesting for this group took place after the fourth session.

The second group was taken to the gym and engaged in a high-activity game of basketball. The subjects in this group were encouraged to run, throw the ball, and to rid themselves of as much energy as they could. This group spent 45 minutes in this strenuous activity before being observed for the second time. The subjects in this physical activity group were observed right after the activity. The effects of physical activity on decreasing hyperactivity should be relatively the same after each session, as it is based on tiring the subjects. The third group remained in the classrooms and was monitored at two different times. This group acted as the control group.

Groups were observed and monitored as in the pretest situation. Again, the observers were not aware of the treatment given each group, but familiarity with the subjects may have led to speculation on group assignments.

RESULTS

The means and standard deviations for each treatment group were calculated from the results of the pretest and posttest hyperactivity checklist (see Table 1).

Analysis of covariance using pretest results as the covariant determined if there were any differences between the treatment groups following treatment. Differences in the pretest scores of groups, used as the covariate, indicated adjusted posttreatment

TABLE 1
Hyperactive Scores* Before and After Treatment

Treatment	Pretest		Posttest		Change	
	Mean	SD	Mean	SD	Mean	SD
Relaxation	16.1	6.8	6.8	3.2	–9.3	4.6
Physical activities	14.7	4.9	9.8	5.3	–4.9	2.6
Control	8.7	2.7	9.5	9.5	–0.8	4.0

*Lower scores represent less hyperactive behavior.

scores were significantly different ($F(3,26)=8.8, p=.00012$). Subjects exposed to relaxation therapy evidenced the greatest decrease in hyperactive behavior. One further step was taken in the analysis. Adjusted change scores (least square means) were contrasted between the three treatments employed in this study. As can be seen in Table 2, relaxation therapy elicited significantly greater changes than either no treatment or physical activity.

TABLE 2
Differences in Adjusted Pretest to Posttest Scores between Groups

Contrast	Change score differences	Probability of real differences when corrected for pretest scores
relaxation vs. control	10.1	.0003
relaxation vs. physical	4.4	.0136
physical vs. control	5.7	.0593

DISCUSSION

The results indicate that there is a difference among the relaxation therapy, physical activity, and control groups. The difference between mean scores, indicates that significant differences occurred between the relaxation therapy and both the physical activity group and the control group.

A major finding of this study was the decrease in hyperactive behavior in the relaxation group as compared to the physical activity group. Significantly greater decreases in hyperactive behavior were observed in the group experiencing relaxation. Releasing energy through a program of vigorous activity has been cited earlier as an effective approach. An approach other than tiring is necessary to explain the effect of relaxation on hyperactivity. The decreased levels of activity were not the result of residual fatigue after exercise. It is possible that the relaxation period was pleasurable and, as a result, the participants sought this state in the period following the formal relaxation program. Clearly, further research is needed to identify why relaxation was effective.

It should be noted that the control group had a low number of hyperactive responses, both the first and the second time it was monitored, compared to the two treatment groups. However, the responses remained consistent between the two observations of the group. According to the measurement instrument, no responses on the checklist indicates a lack of hyperactive behavior. Thus, even though this group had a lower number of responses, posttest responses could have conceivably dropped if a treatment had been given.

There seems to be a general lack of research in controlling hyperactive behavior in mentally retarded populations. More studies are needed to provide information to parents and other professionals who deal with hyperactive, mentally retarded individuals. Further research is needed in the area of programming that decreases hyperactivity in individuals. It would also be interesting to discover how long particular programs must be in effect before a significant decrease in hyperactive behavior is seen. The length of time a program deters future hyperactive responses is another area that should be studied. Programs could be developed that decrease hyperactivity for both long and short periods of time and that could be self-administered.

The results of this study indicate that professionals may use relaxation therapy to decrease hyperactivity in mentally retarded individuals. The greatest harm to both the mentally retarded individual and the leader is to ignore the hyperactive behavior and to provide no program to try to effect a decrease in this type of behavior.

REFERENCES

Allen, K. E., Henke, L. B., Harris, F. R., Baer, D. M., & Reynolds, N. J. (1967). Control of hyperactivity by social reinforcement of attending behavior.

Journal of Educational Psychology, 58, 231–237.
Ayllon, T., Layman D., Kandel, J. J. (1975). A behavioral educational alternative to drug control of hyperactive children. *Journal of Applied Behavioral Analysis, 8,* 137–146.
Berkson, G., Davenport, R. K. (1962). Stereotyped movements of mental defectives. *American Journal of Mental Deficiency, 66,* 849–852.
Cunningham, C. E., & Barkley, R. A. (1979). Interactions of normal and hyperactive children with their mothers in free play and structured tasks. *Child Development, 50,* 217–224.
Day, R. C., & Sadek, S. (1982). The effect of Benson's Relaxation Response on the anxiety levels of Lebanese children. *Journal of Experimental Child Psychology, 34,* 350–356.
Doubros, S. G., & Daniels, G. J. (1966). An experimental approach to the reduction of overactive behavior. *Behavior Research Therapy, 4,* 251–258.
Firestone, P., Peters, S., Rivier, M., & Knights, R. (1978). Minor physical anomalies in hyperactive, retarded and normal children and their families. *Journal of Child Psychology and Psychiatry and Allied Disciplines, 19,* 155–160.
Flavell, J. (1973). Reduction of stereotypes by reinforcement of toy play. *Mental Retardation, 11,* 21–23.
Goetyl, U., Grunbers, F., & Berkowitz, B. (1977). Lithium carbonate in management of hyperactive aggressive behavior of the mentally retarded. *Comprehensive Psychiatry, 18,* 599–606.
Halpern, S. (1978). *Ancient Echoes.* Belmont, CA: Halpern Sounds.
Harvey, J. R. (1979). The potential of relaxation training for the mentally retarded. *Mental Retardation, 17,* 71–76.
Lahey, B., Stempnick, M., Robinson, E., Tyroler, M. (1978). Hyperactivity and learning disabilities as independent dimensions of child behavior problems. *Journal of Abnormal Psychology, 87,* 333–340.
Marholin, D. (1979). The effects of progressive muscle relaxation on the behavior of autistic adolescents: A preliminary analysis. *Child Behavior Therapy, 1,* 75–84.
Mash, E., & Johnston, C. (1982). A comparison of mother and child interactions of younger and older hyperactive and normal children. *Child Development, 53,* 1371–1381.
Morris, R., & Dolker, M. (1974). Developing cooperative play in socially withdrawn retarded children. *Mental Retardation, 12,* 24–27.
O'Leary K., Pelham, W., Rosenbaum, A., & Price G. (1976). Behavioral treatment of hyperkinetic children: An experimental evaluation of its usefulness. *Clinical Pediatrics, 15,* 510–515.
Paloutzian R., Hasazi, J., Streifel, J., & Edgar, C. (1971). Promotion of positive social interaction in severely retarded young children. *American Journal of Mental Deficiency, 75,* 519–524.
Pelham, W. (1981). Attention deficits in hyperactive and learning-disabled children. *Exceptional Education quarterly, 2,* 13–23.
Rickard, H. C., Thrasher, K. A., & Elkins, P. D., (1984). Responses of persons who are mentally retarded to four components of relaxation instruction. *Mental Retardation, 22*(5), 248–252.
Wade, M. G. (1973). Biorhythm and activity level of institutionalized Mentally retarded persons diagnosed hyperactive. *American Journal of Mental Deficiency, 78,* 262–267.

10

MOTORIZED AND SELF-PROPELLED RECREATIONISTS: A COMPARISON ON SELECTED CHARACTERISTICS AND OPINIONS

Timothy D. Schroeder

Motorized and self-propelled recreationists often come into conflict over use of wildlands. This study examines the characteristics and opinions of these two recreational groups through analysis of existing data collected in Oklahoma. The results show the two groups to be more similar than different on the variables measured, leading to a discussion of approaching the conflict problem through improved communication and education rather than through regulation.

Recreational land in the United States is becoming increasingly scarce, and increased recreational use has resulted in increased conflicts among recreational user groups. Outdoor recreation areas are particularly vulnerable to conflicts because it is in those areas that some seek solitude and freedom, but others have differing interpretations of what the area should offer. Noe, Wellman, and Buhyoff (1981) noted that "nowhere has recreation conflict been more evident in recent years than in those areas where motorized and nonmotorized recreationists mix" (p. 223).

Over the last decade the utilization of public lands for recreation by off-road vehicle (ORV) users has risen continuously (McCool, 1977). Badaracco (1976) estimated that there were over seven million ORVs operated in the United States in 1976 with an increase in production predicted. Woosley (1970) reported that 1970 Gallup poll showed that 1 out of every 10 American households owned a motorcycle. This increase in ORV use on public lands has introduced new problems for land managers and an increase in the conflict between ORV users and nonusers.

Because ORV users are very mobile and not confined to developed recreation areas, the occurrence of resource management problems such as littering, noise, vandalism, trail deterioration, vegetation damage, and soil disturbance has become more widely distributed. The vast amount of land used by ORV enthusiasts often makes it difficult to patrol these lands for violators, even though the magnitude of violations may be no more than what occurs in established campgrounds (Peine, 1972). Land managers must also deal with the visitor management problems caused by ORVs, such as the growing and often intense conflict between users and nonusers.

Badaracco (1976) observed that there are certain forms of recreation that are naturally incompatible, one of the most common being the conflict between self-propelled recreationists (cross-country skiers, hikers) and ORV users. Both groups of recreationists require large amounts of space, but often for different reasons and with different expectations. Various studies of ORV users and other recreationists have shown that this conflict is often one-sided. ORV enthusiasts can quickly dominate the area and spoil the pleasures of hikers and cross-country skiers, although the reverse is seldom true. While the ORV is capable of completely destroying the solitary, quiet experience in the natural environment sought by other users, the ORV user is often unaware of the presence of the other users. (McCool, 1977).

Two groups of recreationists who enjoy conflicting activities are snowmobilers and cross-country skiers. Both of these groups engage in their activity during the same season and they both require similar areas. The most common complaints of cross-country skiers against snowmobilers are the noise and lingering fumes caused by the vehicles. Snowmobiles are also capable of destroying the smooth ski tracks needed by skiers and packing the snow which could cause dangerous ruts that can last throughout the winter.

Conflicts have also occurred between other recreation groups. Campers complain that they are often disturbed by the noise and dust created by ORV activity near camping areas. ORVs can destroy the sense of remoteness or the scenery sought after by the hiker. Conflict can even occur between the ORV users themselves, who use their machines to go to remote places and are disturbed by the presence or noise of other machines. Each of these conflicts seem to be occurring because individuals have different interpretations of what recreational areas should offer (Noe et al., 1981).

In order to understand possible conflicts between ORV users and other users of dispersed recreation areas, recreational land managers need to have an understanding of the socioeconomic backgrounds of the user groups and their attitudes and beliefs about recreation and environment. Several studies have provided information of this nature.

Duncan and Maughan (1978) observed that in the controversy over the use of ORVs, it has often been argued that those who use self-propelled forms of travel represent a more elite, wealthy, urban group of people who are not tied down by family, whereas those who use motorized vehicles outdoors are more "average" or "real American." Their Idaho study found that there were few significant socioeconomic differences between nonmotorized and motorized users, although nonmotorized users did have a higher education level. Motorized users were found to have higher family incomes, which was the opposite of what the authors expected (Duncan & Maughan, 1978).

A study of Michigan snowmobilers found that of 3,561 respondents, 25% were skilled workers, 22% were semiskilled, 17% were self-employed, and 11% were professional. The average snowmobiler was 43 years of age, with two children, 12.1 years of formal education, and an annual income of $13,500 (Chubb, 1971).

Knopp and Tyger (1973) speculated that conflicts can occur as a result of basic attitude differences. Their study of snowmobilers and ski tourers in Minnesota found that the two groups had conflicting attitudes on various recreation land management issues. Snowmobilers believed that there should be fewer restrictions placed on recreational uses of land, whereas the ski tourers recognized a need for such restrictions and were more "environmentalist" in their orientations.

THE PROBLEM

The purpose of the study was to investigate the leisure

behavior, recreation and environmental opinions, and demographic characteristics of Oklahoma backpackers and ORV users. By having a better understanding of the similarities and differences between these two groups, recreational land managers will have a better basis for managing dispersed recreation areas where conflicts may arise.

THE DATA

The data analyzed in the study were collected as a part of the 1982 Oklahoma Statewide Comprehensive Outdoor Recreation Plan (SCORP). The SCORP study included telephone interviews with 1,801 randomly selected residents of Oklahoma. During the interviews, representatives of each household were asked their opinions about outdoor recreation and conservation issues, recreation participation patterns in 38 activities, and about the general characteristics of the family.

The subjects of this study were those households which indicated participation in backpacking or ORV use at least once during the previous 12 months. The sample consisted of 51 backpacking and 124 ORV-using households. There were 12 households which participated in both activities and were deleted from the study.

RESULTS

The results of the study indicate that both ORV users and backpackers tended to be active recreationists. When asked whether a member of the household had participated at least once in each of a list of outdoor activities during the previous year, both groups reported high percentages of participation in all types of activities (Table 1). The percentages reported are very similar for the two groups, except for the activities of sailing, tent camping, canoeing, and day hiking, in which more backpackers were active than ORV users.

ORV users participated in ORV riding much more frequently than backpackers backpacked. ORV users reported a median participation of 14.0 days during the previous year (mean = 45.9). Backpackers reported a median participation of 4.5 days (mean = 12.13). See Table 2.

TABLE 1
Percent of Sample Reporting Household Participation during Previous Year

Activity	ORV users (*N*=51)	Backpackers (*N*=124)	Total sample (*N*=1,801)
Swimming	82.3	84.3	53.8
Horseback riding	43.1	39.2	21.7
Picnicking	83.1	80.4	67.8
Bicycling	71.8	78.4	47.8
Backpacking	0.0	100.0	3.7
Motorized boating	58.1	47.1	29.4
Sail boating	5.7	9.8	2.6
Tent camping	29.0	51.0	15.8
Vehicle camping	30.7	25.5	16.0
Canoeing	12.9	37.3	7.6
Day hiking	22.6	43.1	10.2
Fishing	73.4	66.7	50.7
Hunting	54.0	31.4	24.1
Water skiing	39.8	33.3	16.6
ORV use	100.0	0.0	7.6
Visit state parks	47.2	58.8	37.0

Not surprisingly, ORV users also reported higher dollar expenditures than backpackers for the previous year's participation. The ORV users reported a median expenditure of $50.31 (mean = $337.27) while the backpackers reported a median expenditures of $30.00 (mean = $120.65). See Table 2.

Backpackers appeared to have more leisure time than ORV users as measured by several questions. More backpackers (87.3%) took vacations during the previous year than ORV users (72.1%). Backpackers also reported more days paid vacation per year (mean = 10.95) than ORV users (mean = 8.9). More backpackers (72.6%) reported taking weekend trips during the previous year than ORV users (67.7%), and backpackers reported shorter mean workweeks than ORV users, 4.6 days and 5.5 days respectively. See Table 3.

ORV users were much more likely to report participating at a privately owned area than backpackers. More than one half (52.9%) of the ORV users reported a private area as their primary place of participation which is probably partly due to a lack of government areas open to ORVs in Oklahoma. Backpackers were split between

TABLE 2
Degree of Participation in Chosen Activity

Measure of Participation	ORV users ($N=124$)	Backpackers ($N=51$)
Number of days of participation past year		
Five or fewer days	29.4%	57.6%
Ten or fewer days	47.1%	80.3%
Twenty or fewer days	64.7%	90.9%
100 or fewer days	86.0%	97.0%
Median number of days	14.0	4.5
Mean number of days	45.9	12.13
Amount of money spent on activity previous year		
Median dollars	$50.31	$30.00
Mean dollars	$337.27	$120.65

TABLE 3
Amount of Leisure Time Available by Activity

Type of leisure time	ORV users	Backpackers
Percent who took weekend trips during previous year	67.7	72.6
Mean number of days of paid vacation	8.9	10.9
Mean number of days in work week	5.5	4.6

federal, state, and private areas. ORV use was reported as being a close to home activity, with a mediam distance for the primary area being 7.17 miles. Backpackers had a median distance of 100.0 miles to their primary locale of participation.

In terms of demographic characteristics, the backpackers and ORV users were very similar. See Table 4. Income, age, racial makeup, and number of children were nearly identical for the two groups. The major differences were in education, occupational

TABLE 4
Demographic Characteristics of ORV Users and Backpackers in the Sample

Characteristic	ORV users	Backpackers
Mean age of head of household	36.3	39.0
Mean number of children in household	1.7	1.4
Percent of households with married couple	87.9	70.0
Percent of minority households	7.3	5.9
Mean years of education of head of household	13.0	14.6
Occupation of head of household (percent)		
White collar	33.1	51.5
Blue collar	64.0	37.9
Not employed	2.9	10.6
Annual Household Income (percent)		
Under $10,000	7.3	10.8
$10,000 to 14,999	15.5	8.1
$15,000 to 19,999	20.0	24.3
$20,000 to 29,999	25.4	32.5
$30,000 and higher	31.8	24.3

status, and marital status. ORV users had lower educational levels, were more likely to be blue-collar workers, and were more likely to be married than backpackers.

In terms of their opinions about recreation and environmental issues, the two groups were very similar. See Table 5. Both groups rated outdoor recreation as very important to their households; they both thought it was very important for the state to protect natural resources and that the state was doing a good job of protecting them; and they had statistically equivalent levels of

TABLE 5
Attitudes and Opinions of ORV Users and Backpackers

Question	Mean rating ORV Users	Mean rating Backpackers	Significance
How important are recreation facilities to your household?	4.06	4.10	
How satisfied are you with the recreation opportunities available in Oklahoma?	4.05	3.78	
How satisfied are you with the state parks in Oklahoma?	4.11	3.78	*
How important is it for the state parks department to protect natural resources?	4.84	4.67	
How good of a job is the state park department doing of protecting natural resources?	3.99	4.06	

Significance: *Denotes a singificance difference between the groups (0.5 level)
Scale: All responses to the above questions were on a 1 to 5 Likert scale, with 1 being the lowest level of satisfaction or importance and 5 being the highest level of importance or satisfaction.

satisfaction with recreation opportunities available in Oklahoma. The ORV users, however, were being more satisfied with the state parks in Oklahoma than backpackers.

A final characteristic measured was affiliation with organizations. None of the backpackers and very few ORV users belong to environmental groups and less than 15% of either group belongs to an outdoor club.

DISCUSSION

Although conflicts between motorized and nonmotorized recreationists is well documented in the literature, there appears to be more in common between backpackers and ORV users than might be expected. Both groups are active in a wide variety of activities, have similar opinions on resource and recreation issues, and have some similar demographic characteristics.

The major differences between the two groups may point out some of the causes of conflict. First of all, the backpackers have higher educational levels and are more likely to be whitecollar workers—supporting the elitist idea. This elite group might be intolerant of other users (such as ORV users) with "less refined" recreational interests.

Secondly, the backpackers apparently have a greater time commitment to their activity, so they may be intolerant of intrusions. With a median travel distance of 100 miles to their favorite backpacking location, the commitment of travel time would result in a high level of disappointment when confronted with an activity in conflict with their recreational goals. Thus backpackers might feel the need for assurance that conflicts would not occur before investing time and money in travel.

The results of the study suggested several new approaches to dealing with conflict between ORV users and backpackers. The typical approach to the problem has been to set aside certain areas for nonmotorized use which, of course, requires regulation of ORV users. Because of limitations on enforcement capability, this regulation has been attempted mainly through posting and educational efforts. Because backpackers are more highly educated and thus would be more influenced by educational efforts, programs could be directed toward shifting their participation away from high-conflict areas to alternate locations.

The lack of affiliation with outdoor clubs and environmental groups points out the difficulty of finding a forum to discuss ORV use issues. Neither user groups is adequately represented in existing organizations. ORV groups have been cooperative in developing regulations for ORV use on public lands, but they represent a small prcentage of the ORV users. Backpackers are equally difficult to communicate with through established organizations. To solve the problem, communications must be opened, which will require a forum for discussion of the issues with broad representation.

The two groups were not very divergent on their overall attitudes toward the environment. Both supported the need to protect natural resources and had similar opinions of how well the state was doing that. The main cause of conflict would seem to be a lack of understanding of the goals and values of the other group's activity. Shelby (1980) found that participation in both motorized and nonmotorized raft trips made it possible for rafters to describe the advantages and disadvantages of each. Perhaps a program aimed at broadening the range of people's outdoor experiences would develop far greater understanding of the needs and rights of others.

REFERENCES

Badaracco, R. J. (September 1976). ORVs: Often rough on visitors. *Parks and Recreation*, 32–35.

Chubb, M. (Ed.). *Proceedings of the 1971 snowmobile and off the road vehicle research symposium.* Michigan State Agricultural Experiment Station Tech Report No. 8, 1971. Cited in R. L. Bury, *Off-road recrea-vehicles: Research results, administrative studies, and technical articles*, 1970–1975. Council of Planning Librarians, Exchange Bibliography No. 1067.

Duncan, D., & Maughan, R. (1978). Feet vs. ORVs: Are there social differences between back-country users? *Journal of Forestry, 76*, 478–480.

Knopp, T. B., & Tyger, J. D. (1973). A study of conflict in recreational land use: snowmobiling vs. ski-touring. *Journal of Leisure Research*, 5, 6–17.

McCool, S. F. (1977). Perspectives on managing the off-road recreation vehicle. *Western Wildlands*, 4(2), 26–31.

Noe, F. P., Wellman, J. D., & Bohyoff, G. (1981). Perception of conflict between off-road vehicle and non off-road vehicle users in a leisure setting. *Journal of Environmental Systems*, 11(3), 223–233.

Peine, J. D. (1972). *Land management for recreational use of off-road vehicles.* Ph.D. dissertation, University of Arizona.

Shelby, B. (1980). Contrasting recreational experiences: Motors and oars in Grand Canyon. *Journal of Soil and Water Conservation*, 35, 129–131.

Woosley, B. (1970). Incidence of ownership of motorcycles. The Gallup Organization, Inc. Cited in R. J. Badaracco, (September 1976). ORVs: Often rough on visitors. *Parks and Recreation*, 32–35.

11

A LONGITUDINAL ANALYSIS OF ACTIVITIES, CHOICES AND CONSTRAINTS: 1960 AND 1983

J.T. O'Leary
F.A. McGuire
F.D. Dottavio

Important and preferred activities from the 1960 and 1983 Nationwide Outdoor Recreation Surveys are compared. Changes in the rank of activities and in the limitations reported for not doing an activity as often as one would like are described. There have been changes in the number of activities being identified as important, an increase in the percent of people reporting they are unable to do activities as often as they would like, but similarities in the limitations identified. Possible reasons for the changes include technology innovation, media intervention, socioeconomic and demographic change, and alterations in the supply opportunities provided.

Collection of data for the 1960 Outdoor Recreation Resources Review Commission (ORRRC) was an important benchmark in the examination of patterns of recreation behavior in the United States. The ORRRC reports emphasized that outdoor recreation was a pervasive phenomenon pursued by millions of people. However, analyses done by people like Mueller and Gurin (1962) emphasized that participation was not necessarily an egalitarian opportunity. There were differences in activities and constraints that could be addressed in policy development, planning, and management. The recommendations made by ORRRC set in motion a number of programs throughout the country that define today's outdoor recreation infrastructure.

Important activities identified in the 1960 survey affected both planning and policy decisions related to the development of recreation. Similarly, those factors identified as constraints formed the basis for programs that would attempt to remove those constraints. Some professionals are suggesting the 1985 Presidential Commission on Americans Outdoors might impact on the infrastructure of outdoor recreation in a way similar to that of the first Commission. Comparative information between recreation pursuits and constraints from 1960 to the 1980s give us a relevant frame of reference on changes over the past 25 years and so form a basis for future direction and policy.

At the 1985 National Outdoor Recreation Trends Symposium, the importance of looking at recreation change was underscored. A persistent upward trend (but at a decreasing rate) in visitation to public recreation areas (Clawson, 1985); a democratization of leisure travel and an increased role of the private sector (Van Doren, 1985); alteration in leisure ethic and life-style, worklife, and attitudes; a rise in dual-income households; aging of the population; budget and funding constraints; and technological change (Hornback, 1985; O'Leary, 1985) were examples of issues identified that impact on recreation and leisure opportunities. The form of recreation in the future will partially resemble the inheritance from the past. It is thus useful to examine how that inheritance has been changing by looking at measures of recreation involvement, important recreation activities, and common constraints.

In this paper we contrast data collected nationwide in 1960 and 1983 to identify changes in important outdoor recreation activities and the constraints to participation associated with these activities.

PROCEDURE

Data Collection

Two national recreation surveys were used in this analysis of trends. The 1960 Outdoor Recreation Resources Review Commission (ORRRC) survey was administered by the Bureau of the Census. Four series of personal interviews of persons 12 years of age or older ($N = 17{,}752$) were conducted at the end of each season (Kirschner, 1975). The second survey used was gathered as part of the 1983 Nationwide Recreation Survey (NRS). The NRS was jointly sponsored by the National Park Service, U. S. Forest Service, Administration on Aging, and Bureau of Land Management. The National Park Service coordinated the NRS. Data were collected as a supplement to the National Crime Survey (NCS), an ongoing survey sponsored by the U. S. Department of Justice. The NRS was administered to a sample of individuals ($N = 6{,}720$) 12 years of age or older from the noninstitutionalized United States population. Personal interviews were conducted by trained interviewers working for the United States Bureau of the Census.

Question Selection

Several of the questions asked in 1983 were designed to be analogous to those asked in the 1960 survey so that comparisons and changes over time could be examined. One area of similarity was a question asked about the three most important outdoor recreation activities respondents enjoyed doing ('prefer' was the term used in 1960). In both cases the individual was to indicate any outdoor activity without prompting from the interviewer.

In 1960, the respondents were asked the following questions during each seasonal survey:

1. Thinking of summer (fall, winter, spring) what outdoor activity do you like best (second best, third best)?
2. Do you (the activity) as often as you would like?
3. If no, why don't you (the activity) more often?

In 1983, respondents were asked the following questions during each survey:

1. Are there any outdoor recreation activities that you particularly enjoy doing?
2. What are the three most important to you?
3. Do you (the activity) as often as you would like?
4. If not, which, if any, of these are reasons which kept you from (the activity) more often during the past months?

In the analysis, we examined the overall rank of activities identified most often as preferred (1960) or important (1983), regardless of season or survey. The absolute response associated with each of the activities was obtained, and a ranking based on the results was effected. Since the 1960 data had been based on seasonal responses, the rank order of each seasonal survey was examined to be certain that adding across seasons did not distort the data. Although there were some differences, particularly during the winter season when winter activities rose to their highest level, there was little difference across seasons for the activities that ranked highest or which exhibited the greatest change from 1960 to 1983. Responses to the involvement limitation question were ranked for each of the three activity choices a respondent had the opportunity to select. Eleven specific limitations and an "other" category were listed on the 1983 survey questionnaire. These were developed from an open-ended list of limitations gathered in the 1960 survey. Although these two collection strategies are different, the limitation categories are comparable because one was built from information garnered in the first effort. Thirteen reasons for limiting participation were identified as common between the survey years. Limitations identified but not examined were in the "other" category and noted infrequently. In this paper there was no attempt to examine individual activities; all of the limitations associated with the three activity choices were aggregated.

RESULTS

The ranking of the activites in the two surveys is shown in Table 1. One of the most obvious changes that has taken place since 1960 is the increased number of activities people report as preferred or important. There are simply a larger number of things that people are doing now. This increase in diversity has a clear impact on the relative ranking of many of the activites. One activity not changing position and remaining very popular is fishing. Camping appears to have moved up (11 to 8), as have hunting, bicycling, hiking, and the combined categories of walking for pleasure and nature walks. It would also appear that the category of outdoor games and sports is more difficult to interpret since there has been more attention in people's minds to identify sports like baseball, softball, football, basketball, and soccer separately. In

TABLE 1
Overall Rank of Preferred (1960) and Important (1983) Activities in the Nationwide Recreation Surveys.

Activity	Rank	
	1960	**1983**
Fishing	1	1
Swimming	5	2
Nature walks/Walking for pleasure	7	3
Hunting	8	4
Tennis	—	5
Bicycling	17	6
Golfing	—	7
Camping	11	8
Hiking	15	9
Softball	—	10
Running/Jogging	—	11
Gardening	—	12
Baseball	—	13
Picnics	4	14
Horseback riding	12	15
Basketball	—	16
Football	—	17
Water skiing	18	18
Motorboating	—	18
Snow skiing	16	20
Volleyball	—	21
Sailing	20	23
Canoeing	21	24
Motorcycling	—	25
Soccer	—	26
Driving for pleasure	3	—
Playing outdoor games or sports	2	—
Sightseeing	9	*
Attending outdoor sports events	6	*
Attending outdoor concerts	19	*
Backpacking	—	*
Birdwatching	14	*
ORV driving	*	*
Ice Skating	10	*
XC skiing	—	*

continued

TABLE 1 (continued)

Activity	Rank	
	1960	1983
Snowmobiling	—	*
Sledding	13	*
Hangliding	—	*
Badminton	—	*
Frisbee/Horseshoes	—	*
Roller skating	—	*

*Notation indicates that persons listed these activities but the limited number caused the rank to be lower than 21 for the 1960 data and 26 for the 1983 data.

1983, all of these activities, with the exception of soccer, rank as one of the top 20 favorites. In general, by allowing the identification of these sport activities in the "other" category, there is more information, and it would appear that playing outdoor games and sports has become much more focused in terms of specific selections rather than the broad eclectic designation used in 1960.

Sharp declines in rank are evident for driving for pleasure, attending outdoor sports events, attending outdoor concerts, and sightseeing. The energy crisis may have fueled the decline in driving, although it is still popular. Going to sporting events and concerts both continue to be popular. What may be happening is that other activities now available are more preferred. Swimming, one of the most popular activities in 1960, moved up in rank when the two parts (pool and other) from the 1983 survey were combined. Picnicking declined in the overall ranking in 1983. Again, it does not appear that people are doing less, but that activity shifts are occurring.

The activities added to the list by respondents in the 1983 survey, as noted earlier in the discussion of attending outdoor sports events, point toward an expansion of the important activity spectrum. Golf, tennis, jogging/running, and gardening have entered into the 15 most popular choices noted in 1983. Other game-type sports like volleyball, badminton, and frisbee/horseshoes also appear in the top 20 choices identified by the respondents. Off-road vehicle driving, snowmobiling, and motorcycling also appear, although ranked somewhat lower on the list than the other activities noted earlier. What is interesting about motorcycling is that it is in the highest position of the motorized type activities identified in this part of the survey.

Amount of Participation

One of the questions about participation is whether people perceive that they are able to participate as often as they would like in the activities they identify as most important or preferred. Remember, though, more choices are perceived to be available in 1983. Table 2 describes the percentage of people who indicated the ability to actually do their three most preferred outdoor recreation activities. For the most preferred, there has been a decline from 34.3% in 1960 to 29.5% in 1983 in the number of people reporting they are able to do the identified activity as often as they would like. Similarly, for each of the other activity choices, a decrease is apparent in the percentage of respondents indicating they are able to do these activities as often as they would like.

TABLE 2
Percentage of Respondents Indicating Ability to do the Activity as Often as One Likes for the Three Most Preferred Outdoor Recreation Activities

Activity	Yes Responses	
	1960	1983
First choice	34%	29%
Second choice	42%	33%
Third choice	45%	36%

Factors Limiting Participation

Thirteen specific items were identified in the two surveys as limitations that prevented persons from doing the activities they identified as most important or preferred (Table 3). For each of the activities the rank of the three most limiting constraints in 1960 continue to be the most limiting nearly 25 years later. Apparently people still find time, transportation, and monetary limitations the key constraints to participation.

In 1960 there was a great deal of similarity among the rankings of limitations across the three activity choices. However, there are some changes evident in 1983. First, "health" has moved down the list as a limiting factor from fourth to sixth position. Moving up to fourth position is "lack of companions." Perhaps one of the most interesting changes is that "crowding" has moved up to fifth from seventh position. Additionally, "age" as a limiting factor has disappeared as an identified reason in the 1983 survey. Finally, "fear of activity" no longer appears as a limiting factor in the second and third activity lists.

TABLE 3
Rank of Factors Limiting Participation in the Three Most Preferred Outdoor Recreation Activities

Limiters	Activity					
	First Choice		Second Choice		Third Choice	
	1960	1983	1960	1983	1960	1983
Not enough time	1	1	1	1	1	1
Trasportation	2	2	2	2	2	2
Money	3	3	3	3	3	3
Health	4	6	4	6	6	6
Lack of companions	5	4	6	4	5	4
Equipment	6	10	5	8	4	7
Crowding	7	5	7	5	7	5
Weather	8	7	8	7	8	8
Age	9	—	9	—	9	—
Lack of opportunity	10	9	10	10	10	10
Family reasons	11	8	11	9	12	9
Skill	12	12	12	11	11	11
Fear of activity	13	11	13	—	13	—

DISCUSSION

Perhaps the most significant change in the identification of important activities over the 25-year period is the increase in the number of activities identified by the respondents. This increase in diversity poses several interesting concerns that must be dealt with in thinking about the development of future recreation programs. In looking at the activities, it is clear that some of the increase is a product of technology change and media intervention. The latter has brought opportunities to the attention of the public as well as suggested with advertising specific choices that could be pursued. The growth in jogging and running in the United States is a good example of a situation in which the media have played an important role. Interest in the activity has been seen as a by-product of the Olympic marathon successes of Frank Shorter in the early and middle seventies—something that the original ORRRC reports could not have anticipated. This created an environment for rapid development of the running industry in the late seventies and early eighties and contributed to a growing interest in fitness. The evolution has led to a number of products now available to persons doing the activity, as well as those who wish to look as if they are doing it.

Technologcical change has also played an important role. For example, hang gliding, identified by some as an important activity in the 1983 survey, was not an opportunity in 1960. Scuba diving was not widely known nor was there much opportunity for the general public to learn how to do the activity in 1960. Although still not done by many, it is now a new opportunity identified by some as a favorite. It would appear that we will continue to see the development of more new and different kinds of equipment for recreation use, and these will affect recreation pursuits. In some instances this will make participation in an activity safer. In other cases it will tax the regulatory ability of the manager. Small, ultralight planes capable of being carried by one individual and needing only limited space for takeoff and landing make almost all remote and wilderness areas accessible to the thrill seeker. Fishing (still the number one activity in terms of importance) can be done with computerized depth finders and sonar to detect the location of fish. Will this affect the stocking and quality of the experiences? Hiking (one of the more important activities in 1983) and backpacking have been called "new wave" because of the incorporation of new technology and materials to make things lighter and smaller. Will this cause more women and children to move into the activity? Mountain bikes are sturdy, nongasoline powered vehicles that allow one to go off the road. They are also great for urban situations replete with curbs, holes, and grates in the road. No one in 1960 would have even known what a frisbee was, yet today the disc is sold in several sizes, as well as given away as a promotional product. Clearly technology provides more specialized equipment to address the evolution and specialization that goes on with complex activity change. Game sports like volleyball, badminton, and frisbee/horseshoes, which have risen in popularity, will probably continue to exhibit these changes.

Change in the supply of parks, forests, trails, and waterways has also created a setting in which more and different activities can be done. Hof and Kaiser (1983), in discussing the modeling for the U. S. Forest Service RPA program in recreation, suggested that the historical supply trend in the United States has been a 7-percent increase each year in the supply of outdoor recreation areas. By providing more places to participate, the opportunity to do an activity, to participate more times, and to do new things increases. The fact that this increase in supply has occurred makes the constraint response about crowding even more interesting, since it has moved up in the relative rank of limitations that were examined. It would appear that the concern raised by Clawson (1984, 1985) about effective supply is an issue here. There may be more space, but not necessarily in the right place or in the right form to accommodate the growing variety of activities different groups wish to pursue. One of the key findings in these data that must be emphasized is the larger percentage of people in 1983 indicating limitations in doing their important activities in spite of (or maybe as a result of) the changes in supply that have taken place.

A feeling that not enough time is available to do the things we'd like to do has carried over from the 1960s. Changes in the larger society where the majority of married couples are both working and trying to take care of personal needs possibly indicates why this problem remains. A similar problem probably exists for many single-parent families.

With time as a problem, we can anticipate more demand for opportunities close to home and for information about places that maximize satisfaction in the pursuit of outdoor recreation. Looking at the important activities could suggest which areas these demands might focus on. For example, several of the activities that have moved up in rank tend to emphasize linear corridors (bicycling and jogging/running). In addition, with an increase in the diversity of activities, involvement in some of these can be expected to place special demands on recreation areas as people increase their experience, combining the search for quantity and quality. Many activities will have to take place in a supply setting that is either not growing or is expanding at levels less than the rates evident in the last 20 years. The special demands on the settings will require special management that for some will mean the quality of the outdoor experience is less than it has been in the past (Jacob & Schreyer, 1980). More emphasis will be placed on operations and management. When these changes are put in the context of decreasing budgets but increasing complexity of opportunity, future trends in outdoor recreation become even more interesting.

CONCLUSION

In the 25 years since the first ORRRC commission studied the outdoor recreation patterns of the American public, some changes have become apparent in the relative importance and breadth of activities being done. In some instances it is possible to link these to external forces that appear to accelerate change or create an environment in which potential acceleration could take place. Changes in activity preferences as well as increasing diversity in activity repertoires will demand new and creative approaches to the management of outdoor areas. The findings of this study are a first step in providing the data upon which those approaches are to be founded.

REFERENCES

Clawson, M. (Fall, 1984). Effective acreage for outdoor recreation. Resources, Resources for the Future.

Clawson, M. (1985). Trends in the use of public recreation areas. *Proceedings of the National Outdoor Recreation Trends Symposium* II, Myrtle Beach, SC February, 1–12.

Hof, J. G., & Kaiser, H. F. (1983). Long-term outdoor recreation participation projections for public land management agencies. *Journal of Leisure Research,* 15(1), 1–14.

Hornback, K. E. (February 1985).Social trends and leisure behavior. *Proceedings of the National Outdoor Recreation Trends Symposium* II, Myrtle Beach, SC: 37–48.

Jacob, R., & R. Schreyer. (1980). Conflict in outdoor recreation: A theoretical perspective. *Journal of Leisure Research,* 12(4):368–380.

Mueller, E., & Gurin, G. (1962). Participation in outdoor recreation: Factors affecting demand among American adults, study report 20. *Outdoor Recreation Resources Review Commission*, Washington, DC: U. S. Government Printing Office,

Kirschner Associates, Inc. (November 1975). Interim report: Evaluation of five previous nationwide citizen surveys. Washington, DC: Author.

O'Leary, J. T. (1985). Social trends in outdoor recreation. *Proceedings of the National Outdoor Recreation Trends Syumposium* II, Myrtle Beach, SC February, 24–36.

Van Doren, C. S., Social trends and social indicators: The private sector. *Proceedings of the National Outdoor Recreation Trends Symposium* II, Myrtle Beach, SC February, 13–23.

12

FACTORS CONTRIBUTING TO THE SATISFACTION OF WOMEN IN RECREATION PROGRAMS AT SENIOR CENTERS

Sandra L. Hupp

This investigation was an examination of the relationship of leisure satisfaction and leisure attitude to leisure program satisfaction of women aged 55 and older (N = 294). The relationship of age, marital status, life/work status, and living arrangement to leisure program satisfaction, leisure satisfaction, and leisure attitude was also investigated. Three questionnaires—a revised version of the Leisure Program Evaluation Form (Rossman, 1981/1982), the Leisure Satisfaction Scale (Beard & Ragheb, 1980), and the Leisure Attitude Scale (Ragheb & Beard, 1982)—were administered at three senior centers in Oregon during the fall of 1984.

A multiple regression analysis indicated that 31% of the variability of leisure program satisfaction was explained by leisure satisfaction and leisure attitude. Other major findings are

1. *Achievement, Relaxation, and Environment subscales of leisure program satisfaction can be used to predict leisure program satisfaction.*
2. *An apparent trend existed for participants in drop-in programs to have greater program satisfaction than those in other program format (classes, leader-directed, and special events) activities.*
3. *An apparent trend existed for the least satisfaction in leader-*

directed programs.

4. *The oldest group of women (aged 76 and older) had a more positive leisure attitude than the other women.*

One means to gain information about the provision of leisure services and to anticipated future needs and requirements concerning leisure is to assess stated preferences and satisfactions of the public (Chase & Cheek, 1979). Based on such an assessment, public agencies sponsoring senior citizens centers may be able to determine practical implications for the delivery of leisure services, including the demand for various leisure programs for older women.

The National Council on the Aging (1981) indicated that in 1981, as compared to 1974, there was a decline in various social activities,—socializing with friends, watching television, and activities that could be termed nonstructured leisure activities for older adults. There was, however, an increase in older adult involvement in 1981 in structured or organized leisure programs, as evidenced by participation in senior citizens centers and in golden age club, community neighborhood center, and recreation center programs. There were also indications of increased interest, particularly by older women, in senior citizens centers for future years. Information collected from the Harris Survey in 1981 showed that 31% of the women aged 55 or older would like to attend a senior citizens center or golden age club, which is 6% higher than the 1974 figures based on a similar item (National Council on the Aging, 1981).

In addition to understanding sources of satisfaction, leisure service professionals, gerontologists, sociologists, and others (Beard & Ragheb, 1980; Crandall, 1979; DiGrino, 1983; Koss, 1983; MacLean, 1983) are interested in understanding leisure participation, leisure satisfaction, and attitudes of older people toward leisure. Although review of the literature indicates research on activity participation, particularly by frequency of participation, leisure satisfaction, and life satisfaction of older people, there is little evidence of research in these areas specifically focused on the satisfaction of older women in various leisure programs.

Review of the literature with respect to leisure practices among older adults contained information in the three general areas of successful aging and activity participation, life satisfaction with regard to leisure participation, and leisure patterns and preferences in activity participation.

Literature in the areas of leisure satisfaction, leisure attitude, leisure program participation, and leisure studies with older adults was reviewed. Leisure satisfaction is sometimes studied with respect to frequency of participation in leisure activities (Ragheb, 1980). Researchers (Beard & Ragheb, 1980; Hawes, 1978) have suggested that leisure satisfaction obtained from leisure activities is a major factor related to leisure choices. In recent years, Buchanan (1983), Pierce (1980), and Ragheb and Beard (1982) have focused on identifying various dimensions of leisure satisfaction. These researchers support the notion that more than one variable affects or contributes to overall leisure satisfaction and, therefore, research on leisure satisfaction should include the use of a variety of leisure satisfaction dimensions or subscales.

Literature that was cited (Mobley, Light, & Neulinger, 1976; Ragheb & Beard, 1982) indicated positive relationships between degree and frequency of leisure activity participation and leisure attitude. In general, findings (Christensen & Yoesting, 1973; Neulinger & Raps, 1972; Ragheb, 1980) showed that participation in leisure activities was explained more by leisure satisfaction than by leisure attitude.

In recent years, evidence of research with respect to program formats and participation satisfaction has appeared in the literature. Rossman (1981/1982) investigated the influence of five program formats (leader-directed, leagues and tournaments, instructional classes, open facilities, and special events) on participant satisfaction with community recreation department programs and suggested that seven dimensions of leisure satisfaction could be identified.

The purpose of this study was to examine the relationship of leisure satisfaction and leisure attitude to leisure program satisfaction of older women participating in various leisure programs offered by selected senior centers. In addition, the relationships of various selected demographic variables including age, marital status, and life/work status, and living arrangement to leisure program satisfaction, leisure satisfaction, and leisure attitude were investigated.

METHOD

A selected sample of older women completed three questionnaires designed to examine the relationship of leisure satisfaction and leisure attitude to leisure program satisfaction. This sample ($N = 294$), selected by convenience, included women aged 55 and older participating in programs offered by three selected senior centers in the state of Oregon. Each selected center served over 1,000 participants and had program offerings with enrollemnt for the data collection period of at least one program in each of the four program formats: instructional classes, leader directed activities, drop-in, and special events.

The program offering for each of the selected senior centers were categorized into one of four program formats (as indicated by Rossman, using Farrell and Lundegren's formats as guidelines). Programs selected for each of four program formats were purposely selected to ensure representation of a variety of program activities (social, arts, education, and physical fitness) in each format category. Examples of the categories of program formats and activities included the program offerings:

Program	*Format*	*Activity Type*
French	Class	Education
Liquid embroidery	Class	Arts
Hand bell choir	Leader-directed	Arts
Lunch on the coast	Special event	Social
Cribbage	Drop-in	Education
Walking for fun	Drop-in	Physical fitness

Intact program groups were used to facilitate the collection of data; thus, no attempt was made to select subjects randomly. To avoid duplication of sample subjects, participants were asked to respond to the questionnaires only in terms of the program in which they were participating when they received the instrument.

The first three questionnaires of the research instrument consisted of the revised version of the Leisure Program Evaluation Form (Rossman, 1981/1982), the Leisure Attitude Scale (Beard & Ragheb, 1980), and the Leisure Attitude Scale (Ragheb & Beard, 1982). A general participant questionnaire was used to collect specific demographic information regarding age, marital status, life/work status, and living arrangements.

The Leisure Program Evaluation Form by Rossman (1981/1982) was revised and used to measure leisure program satisfaction. With Rossman's instrument, analysis of the results can be made with regard to 10 subscales measuring various aspects of leisure program satisfaction, such as achievement, physical fitness, and social enjoyment. Rossman (1981/1982) reported reliability alphas with a range from .678 to .908 for the subscales; content validity was determined by a jury of leisure service professionals.

Revision of Rossman's instrument resulted in a two-part participant self-report questionnaire. The first section was used to collect information related to leisure program satisfaction. It included 21 questions with an eight-point Likert-type scale response format with the following guidelines (designed by Rossman, 1981/1982) used to interpret the numerical scores:

1. Scores 7 and 6 = very satisfying
2. Scores 5 and 4 = satisfying
3. Scores 3 to 1 = contributing no satisfaction; and
4. Scores 0 = not applicable.

The first 21 items of the revised instrument were used to determine the leisure program satisfaction subscale components following Rossman's guidelines. The subscales were Achievement, Physical Fitness, Social Enjoyment, Family Escape, Environment, Autonomy, Relaxation, and Fun. Subscale scores were obtained by calculating a mean satisfaction score for all of the items in each subscale for each subject.

The second section of the revised Leisure Program Evaluation Form had five questions. These items were used to place overall leisure program satisfaction results in perspective with the importance of the leisure program, frequency of participation, rank of the program compared to all other leisure activities, overall satisfaction with the program, and satisfaction with the leader or supervisor of the program. These data were analyzed descriptively.

To determine overall leisure program satisfaction, Rossman depended on the responses from one single item—"Which of the following statements reflects your overall satisfaction with this program?"—which is Question 25 in the second section of the instrument. The researcher decided that a more reasonable means for determining overall leisure program satisfaction was necessary and, therefore, used the mean score of the 21 items related to leisure program satisfaction.

The Leisure Satisfaction Scale developed by Beard and Ragheb (1980) was used to determine leisure satisfaction. This questionnaire included 24 items and used a five-point Likert-type scale with *almost always true* (score of 5) and *almost never true* (score of 1) as the scale anchors. Total alpha reliability, as reported by Beard and Ragheb (1980), yielded a .96 value, with component parts yielding values between .85 and .92. Content validity was tested by professors, researchers, and practitioners in leisure behavior and recreation. The mean score for leisure satisfaction was computed and used for statistical analyses in this study.

The Leisure Attitude Scale (Ragheb & Beard, 1982) was used to measure participant attitude toward leisure. This questionnaire included 36 items and used a five-point Likert-type scale with *strongly agree* or *always* (score of 5) and *strongly disagree* or *never* (score 1) as the anchors. The alpha reliability coefficient is .94 for the total scale with subscale coefficients ranging between .89 and .93 (Ragheb & Beard, 1982). The mean score for leisure attitude was computed and used for statistical analyses in this study.

The instruments were administered during regularly scheduled leisure programs. Data were collected from women participants in ongoing programs after the fifth week into the scheduled period, which was at least the midpoint of these programs, and before the final session of the scheduled period. Women participating in one-day or one-time programs were selected and surveyed during the same period as other participants for that center.

DATA ANALYSIS

Statistical analyses included the use of descriptive statistics to describe the participants in the study and their program participation. Descriptive statistics were computed for overall leisure program satisfaction, the five subscales (Achievement, Social Enjoyment, Environment, Relaxation, and Fun) of leisure program satisfaction, leisure satisfaction, and leisure attitude.

Information regarding the importance of the leisure program to the individual, the rank of the leisure program compared to all other leisure activities, overall leisure satisfaction indicated by

Question 25, and satisfaction with the leader or supervisor of the leisure program were determined by using the crosstab procedures of SPSS (Statistical Package for the Social Sciences). Research questions were answered using regression analysis and analysis of variance by using the SPSS-X computer program.

During the data collection period, various situations at the centers created difficulties in obtaining data. For some reasons, which the researcher cannot explain, some program activities had a much larger participant response than others. Although the researcher had taken precautions to make the instrument easy to read, there were occasions when more than one response was given or no responses were made. With these issues in mind, the researcher established a 75% criterion for the data to be included in the study. Questionnaires, variables (including leisure program subscales), and statistical procedures had to have at least 75% of completed responses or completed group to be included in the statistical analyses of this study. The 75% criterion affected the following. The eight subscale components of leisure program satisfaction were reduced to five usable subscales including Achievement, Social Enjoyment, Environment, Relaxation, and Fun. Two-way analysis of variance procedures were affected because of the small cell size and the large number of missing data and, therefore, one-way analysis of variance procedures were computed to answer revised research questions.

A total of 294 women completed usable questionnaires. The age range of respondents was 55 to over 76 years of age with over one half (54.8%) of the sample grouped between the ages of 61 and 70 and almost one third (32%) of the participants indicating their age as over 71. These data seem to be consistent with national data which describes typical senior center participants (National Council on the Aging, 1981). Marital status categories indicated that about one half of the sample participants were married and one half nonmarried.

Data regarding life/work status indicated a high percentage (58.2%) of the participants were retired from employment, and 24% of the participants considered themselves as homemakers. Statistics from this study showed that nearly as many women lived alone (n = 131) as women who lived with their husbands (n = 132).

Participants responded to the instrument from the perspective of their satisfaction with the program in which they were participating at the time of data collection. Descriptive information concerning respondent participation by program format was as follows: class, 44.6%; leader-directed, 28.2%; special event, 9.2%; and drop-in, 18%. The combination of class and leader-directed program formats indicated that 72.8% of the respondents were engaged in leader-structured programs. Approximately one half (50.3%) of the participants in this study were involved in an arts type of activity; physical fitness activities had the smallest percentage (11.6%).

Forced-entry multiple regression analysis of leisure attitude and leisure satisfaction, respectively, indicated that 31% of the variance of overall leisure program satisfaction was explained by leisure attitude and leisure satisfaction. See Table 1. Explanation of 31% of the variance is noteworthy considering the nature of the variable leisure program satisfaction.

The set of leisure program satisfaction subscales—Achievement, Social Enjoyment, Environment, Relaxation, and Fun—was regressed, using the SPSS-X stepwise procedure on overall leisure program satisfaction, to determine the dependence of overall leisure program satisfaction on each of the subscales. Results of this procedure indicated that Achievement, Relaxation, and Environment were the best predictors of overall leisure program satisfaction. The multiple R for Achievement, entered on the first step, was .83, indicating that 69% of the variance in overall leisure program satisfaction is explained be Achievement alone. The explained variance of overall leisure program satisfaction with Achievement, Relaxation, and Environment was 92%. The addition of Social Enjoyment and Fun, in that order, merely increased the predictive capabilities by explaining an additional 3% of the variance.

One-way ANOVA procedures were computed to answer the question, "Is there a significant difference in overall leisure program satisfaction when compared by age, marital status, life/work status, and living arrangement?" Results of these analyses indicated that none of the F ratios had a value great enough to reach the .05 level of significance and, therefore, the data showed evidence of no differences in overall leisure program satisfaction with regard to age, marital status, life/work status, and living arrangement.

TABLE 1
Regression to Predict Overall Leisure Program Satisfaction from Leisure Satisfaction and Leisure Attitude

Variable Entered on Step Number 1: Leisure Attitude
Variable Entered on Step Number 2: Leisure Satisfaction

Multiple R	.56
R^2	.31
Standard Error	.68
F Ratio	48.80*
*F2, 200; .05 = 3.04	

Variables in the Equation

Variable	R	B	$SE\ B$	Beta
Leisure Attitude	.51	.58	.15	.30
Leisure Satisfaction	.56	.49	.12	.31
(constant)		1.32	.50	

Note: Dependent Variable = Leisure Program Satisfaction.
*$p < .05$.

One-way ANOVAS were computed to answer the question, "Is there a significant difference in subscale components of leisure program satisfaction when compared by leisure program formats?" Although no significant differences were found with these analyses, a trend for leisure program satisfaction means was apparent. One-way ANOVA computations with leisure program satisfaction subscales and program formats revealed that 80% of the time leader-directed program formats had the lowest mean, and 80% of the time the drop-in leisure program format mean was the highest.

The relationships of leisure satisfaction and the selected demographic variables of age, marital status, life/work status, and living arrangement were investigated. The results of one-way analysis of variance indicated that no differences existed in leisure satisfaction when compared by age, marital status, life/work status, and living arrangement.

The results of one-way ANOVAs to determine differences in leisure attitude when compared by demographic variable resulted in the rejection of the null hypothesis that "no differences exist in leisure attitude means when compared by age, marital status, life/work status, and living arrangement." See Table 2. A signifi-

TABLE 2
One-Way ANOVAs Comparing Demographic Data on Leisure Attitude

Variable[a]	Statistic				
	Mean	*SD*	*n*	*F* Ratio	*p*
Age				2.627	.035*
55–60	4.37	b	.39	21	
61–65	4.37[b]	.46	67		
66–70	4.37[b]	.48	84		
71–75	4.37[b]	.42	51		
76 and older	4.37[c]	.34	30		
Marital Status				.687	.560
Single	4.30	.46	17		
Married	4.40	.44	122		
Divorced/Separated	4.43	.41	19		
Widow	4.33	.47	97		
Life/Work Status				1.339	.255
Homemaker	4.28	.50		64	
Part-Time Employee	4.36	.33	16		
Full-Time Employee	4.58	.63	8		
Retired from Full-Time	4.39	.42	147		
Retired from Part-Time	4.29	.45	19		
Living Arrangement				1.115	.349
Alone	4.36	.43	120		
With Husband	4.39	.45	121		
With Companion	4.31	.61	5		
With Children	3.89	.39	3		
With Relative	4.24	.64	8		

[a]Five-point response scale.
[b]Post hoc analysis means with similar superscripts do not differ significantly at the .05 level.
[c]Post hoc analysis mean differs significantly from age group 66–70 and age group 71–75 at the .05 level.
*$p < .05$.

cant difference did exist among the ages of the sample population. Post-hoc analysis using the Fisher LSD procedure indicated that significant differences existed between the oldest group (76 years and older) and both of the next two age groups (71–75 and 66–70 years of age). It appears that the oldest age group in this sample had the most positive leisure attitude.

RESULTS AND DISCUSSION

In summary, the following are major findings of this study:

1. Leisure satisfaction and leisure attitude seem to contribute to overall leisure program satisfaction of older women participating in senior center programs.
2. Achievement, Relaxation, and Environment subscales of leisure program satisfaction can be used to predict leisure program satisfaction.
3. Participants' overall leisure program satisfaction and leisure satisfaction were high, with no differences regarding age, marital status, life/work status, and living arrangement.
4. An apparent trend existed for those participants in drop-in programs to have greater program satisfaction than those participating in other program format (classes, leader-directed, and special events) activities.
5. An apparent trend existed for least satisfaction in leader-directed programs.
6. The oldest group of women (aged 76 and older) had a more positive leisure attitude than the other women in this study.

Based on the analysis of the data and in view of the research findings, the following conclusions seem warranted. This sample of older women (N = 294) seems to be consistent with national data (National Council on the Aging, 1981) which indicated that senior citizens centers primarily serve older individuals between the ages of 60 and 75. Participants of this study, however, do not typify the generally recognized single or widow description of older women since approximately one half of the sample were married.

By far the largest number of respondents were participating in class-format activities and arts-activity types of leisure programs. The lowest number of repsondents were participants in special event formats and physical fitness types of activities. Practical applications might indicate that senior center personnel involved with programming should review their program offerings with regard to program format and activity type. It may be that these results are indications of the needs and desires of senior center participants at only these three centers. The possibility may exist, however, that there are not many opportunities for special events or physical fitness activities. The programs offered could reflect the programmer's desires or stereotypical ideas regarding activities and programs for older adults.

In this study a significant amount of the variance (31%) in overall leisure program satisfaction was explained by leisure satisfaction and leisure attitude. Researchers in the past have discussed various aspects of satisfaction with leisure in broad and general terminology. Some current researchers (Beard & Ragheb, 1980; Ragheb & Beard, 1982; Ragheb & Griffith, 1982; Rossman, 1981/1982) are advocating use of subscales to provide more definitive information regarding the general areas of satisfaction. Data from this study indicate that three subscales of leisure program satisfaction—Achievement, Relaxation, and Environment—explained 92% of the variance of overall leisure program satisfaction. Programmers at the three centers involved in this study might examine leisure programs to determine those programs that can provide opportunities for participants to experience these areas of satisfaction with regard to leisure programs.

With respect to leisure program format, drop-in programs had the highest mean scores, and leader-directed programs consistently (80% of the time) had the lowest mean scores for leisure program satisfaction. An implication for leisure programmers at the three centers is that the nature of leader-directed programs should be further investigated. It may be that the older women participating in these programs prefer a less structured leader-type of activity. The respondents were more satisfied with self-directed types of activities.

No significant differences were found regarding leisure satisfaction when compared by age, marital status, life/work status, and living arrangement. The data of this study showed leisure satisfaction was very high, regardless of age; married or non-married; retired, employed, or homemaker; or living alone or with someone. Are there other sociodemographic characteristics that do influence program satisfaction? Since these demographic variables indicated no differences in overall leisure program satisfaction, what then are the aspects or dimensions that made these women so satisfied with leisure and the leisure programs in which they were participating? Other variables such as meaning of leisure, attitudes toward retirement and aging, amount of leisure time, and with whom people spend their leisure time might be considered for future investigation.

Significant differences in leisure attitude were found regarding the age of the women studied. The oldest women (76 years and older) had the highest mean score for leisure attitude. The attitudes of the oldest women were significantly different from those of the women aged 71 to 75 and women aged 66 to 70, but not from those aged 55 to 65. Perhaps the oldest age group has had enough time to becoome comfortable with the leisure lifestyle they are living and, therefore, they have a more positive attitude toward leisure than the women aged 66 to 75. The findings of no difference in leisure attitude between the young-old (ages 55 to 65) and the old-old (ages 76 and above) can not be explained in this study.

Senior center directors and personnel involved with programming for the three centers could utilize these study findings in the planning and implementation of leisure programs. Programs offered at the centers should provide opportunities for participants to have positive experiences in the areas of achievement, relaxation, and environment. Participants indicated greater satisfaction with drop-in programs as compared to leader-directed programs; however, a review of the program offerings at the centers showed that more programs were offered with a leader-directed format than with a drop-in program format.

From the data of this study, it appears that leader satsifaction may be an important consideration in leisure program satisfaction. The relationship of the program leader and the program format might be important to consider when preparing program offerings at these centers.

Regarding the type of activities offered at the senior centers, center directors and programmers may wish to investigate the programs considered important to participants. Those persons involved with senior center programming may want to survey center participants to determine if the programs presently offered are in fact the only programs desired by participants or if there are other programs that might be more satisfying.

Several issues still remain for further research concerned with participant satisfaction with leisure programs. Further research regarding leisure program satisfaction could include investigation of participation in other organized leisure programs, such as municipal recreation centers and community retirement centers, as well as self-initiated leisure activities. The researcher recommends that further research with older adults (including both men and women) on leisure program satisfaction, leisure satisfaction, and leisure attitude should include individuals who do not participate in senior center programs and those individuals who drop out of programs or who do not attend on a regular basis.

REFERENCES

Beard, J. G., & Ragheb, M. G. (1980). Measuring leisure satisfaction. *Journal of Leisure Research, 12*, 20–30.

Buchanan, T. (1983). Toward an understanding of variability in satisfactions within activities. *Journal of Leisure Research, 15*, 39–51.

Chase, D. R., & Cheek, N. H. (1979). Activity preferences and participation: Conclusions from a factor analytic study. *Journal of Leisure Research, 11*, 92–101.

Christensen, J., & Yoesting, D. (1973). Social and attitudinal variants in high and low use of outdoor recreational facilities. *Journal of Leisure Research, 5*, 6–15.

Crandall, R. (1979). Social interaction, affect and leisure. *Journal of Leisure Research, 11*, 165–181.

DiGrino, B. N. (1983). Role of leisure in physical and mental health. In National Recreation and Park Association, *Aging and leisure* (pp. 74–77). Alexandria, VA: Author.

Hawes, D. K. (1978). Satisfaction derived from leisure-time pursuits: An exploratory nationwide survery. *Journal of Leisure Research, 10*, 247–264.

Koss, R. S. (1983). Aging and health—Changing life styles. In National Recreation and Park Association, *Aging and leisure* (pp. 30–43). Alexandria, VA: Author.

MacLean, J. R. (1983). Too hot in the kitchen sociological environments for older Americans. In National Recreation and Park Association, *Aging and leisure* (pp. 15–29). Alexandria, VA: Author.

Mobley, T. A., Light, S. S., & Neulinger, J. (1976). Leisure attitudes and program participation. *Parks and Recreation, 11*(12), 20–22.

National Council on the Aging. (1981). *Aging in the eighties: America in transition*. Washington, DC: Author.

Neulinger, J. & Raps, C. (1972). Leisure attitudes of an intellectual elite. *Journal of Leisure Research, 4*, 196–207.

Pierce, R. C. (1980). Dimensions of leisure. I. Satisfactions. *Journal of Leisure Research, 12*, 5–19.

Ragheb, M. G. (1980). Interrelationships among leisure participation, leisure

satisfaction and leisure attitudes. *Journal of Leisure Research, 12,* 138–149.
Ragheb, M. G., & Beard, J. G. (1982). Measuring leisure attitude. *Journal of Leisure Research, 14,* 155–167.
Ragheb, M. G., & Griffith, C. A. (1982). The contribution of leisure participation and leisure satisfaction to life statisfaction of older people. *Journal of Leisure Research, 14,* 295–306.
Ray, R. O. (1979). Life satisfaction and activity involvement: Implications for leisure service. *Journal of Leisure Research, 11,* 112–119.
Rossman, J. R. (1982). Development of a leisure program evaluation instrument (Doctoral dissertation, University of Illinois at Urban-Champaign, 1981). *Dissertion Abstracts International, 42,* 4146A.

13

HEALTH RELATED IMPACTS OF A MUSIC PROGRAM ON NURSING HOME RESIDENTS

Carol Cutler Riddick
Mary Ellen Dugan-Jendzejec

The purposes of this study were to examine the impact of a music program on the affect balance, self-concept, and verbal interactions of nursing home residents. There were 10 individuals in the experimental group and 14 persons in the control group. The music program consisted of 12 sessions held once a week for 30 minutes a session. The experimental group, relative to the control group, experienced a significant change in affect balance. Neither group, however, underwent a significant alteration in self-concept. The experimental group did, over the course of the music program, undergo a substantial and significant increase in verbal interactions. Ideas for future research and practice are discussed.

Burnside (1978) suggests that one of the fundamental responsibilities of geriatric activity professionals is to develop programs that are designed to lessen the impact of sensory deprivation with the aging process. It has further been noted that appropriate treatment objectives for therapeutic recreators, working with geriatric populations, include maintaining or improving psychological and social health (Bright, 1972; Tanner & O'Briant, 1980).

One medium for meeting these treatment objectives has been to offer music-related programs. Among the claims for using music in a therapeutic milieu is that it can motivate even the most depressed person, improve self-esteem, and stimulate social interaction (Douglass, 1978; Gaston, 1968). Several studies tend to support these assertions. Reigler (1980) noted that the therapeutic use of music led to improvement of elderly persons' reality orientation and hence affected their psychological well-being. Meseck (1978) and Wolfe (1983) have also reported that the use of music with geriatric populations resulted in improved mental status. In addition, Phillips (1980) maintains that geriatric patients who attended music therapy sessions allegedly experienced a fostering of self-concept. Similarly, Wolfe (1983) reported that geriatric patients participating in a music program, compared to a control group, showed marked improvement on a questionnaire that included items measuring attitudes towards self. Moreover, the impact of group music activity in interpersonal relationships among elderly institutionalized persons has also been examined (Hennessey, 1978). Cassity (1976), for example, found that such an activity had a significant positive influence on group interaction.

In reviewing the research literature on how music can affect the lives of elderly persons, three points must be made. First, there is a paucity of research on the subject. There simply is not a substantial body of literature that reports on the responses of institutionalized elderly persons to music programs. Second, the few studies that have been conducted on the topic frequently suffer from methodological inadequacies, including failure to collect baseline (or pretest) data and/or the exclusion of a comparative (or control) group. Third, earlier works on the subject can be characterized as being atheoretically based. Nonetheless, it would seem that a suitable paradigm to steer research in this area is the activity theory (Atchley, 1977). Basically, this theory posits a positive relationship between activity and successful aging, as measured by various proxy measures of psychological and social health.

Consequently, in order to contribute to the knowledge base,

the purposes of this study were to examine the effects of a music program on two aspects of psychological health (affect balance and self concept), as well as on social health (the verbal interactions of nursing home residents). Using the activity theory, it is hypothesized that:

1. Music program participants, relative to a control group, would undergo a significant and positive change in affect balance.
2. Music program participants, relative to a control group, would experience a significant and positive change in self-concept.
3. Over the course of participating in the music program, the nursing home residents would experience a significant increase in verbal interactions.

PROCEDURES

Sample

The nonequivalent control group design was employed for testing the first two hypotheses, and a one-group pretest-posttest design was used for testing the third hypothesis. Subjects for the study were drawn from two different nursing homes, because the site selected for the experiemental intervention did not have a sufficient number of residents to be involved in the study. The two homes involved in the investigation were owned by the same proprietary extended care organization. The daily charge for residents at both facilities was between $55 and $71. Services provided for this fee, and throughout the conduct of the study, included nursing care, meals, recreational activities, and housekeeping. Prior to the conduct of the study, described herein, both nursing homes had offered music programs to their residents. At the time the study was initiated (January 1982), however, only one home was offering a music-related program, and so this home served as the source for experimental group members.

Criteria used for selecting individuals for the study were as follows: they were residents of the nursing home; 60 years of age or older; not bedridden; judged, on a subjective basis, by the therapeutic recreation professional at the facility as being mentally competent; and gave their informed written consent for participating in the study. Initially 36 persons (or 18 individuals each in the experimental and control groups) were identified as participants in the study. At the conclusion of the study, complete information was available for only 10 members of the experimental group and 14 members of the control group. The attrition rate was due principally to deaths and discharges to hospitals, other nursing homes, or the community.

Treatment

The music program consisted of 12 sessions, held once a week for 30 minutes per session. Each program was conducted by two graduate-level students as part of a course requirement at Catholic University in Washington, D.C. Both instructors already had a bachelor's degree in music, had previous experience in leading music programs with nursing home residents, and were pursuing course work that would make them eligible for Registered Music Therapist status through the National Association for Music Therapy.

The music program sessions were held in the activities room of the nursing home. Structurally the program relied on didactic presentations and group play, involvement, and discussions. Leadership approaches used included reality, reminiscence, and remotivation techniques. Examples of activities conducted in the 12 sessions are of group and round singing combined with scarf exercises; nonmusical notation using rhythm instruments; bean bag musical Tic Tac Toe (or a combination of "Name That Tune," and "Tic Tac Toe" games); canon and Haiku writing; bell, autoharp, and Orff instrument playing; and presentations and group discussions on the impressionistic period in music, operas, symphonies, and big band music. Detailed information on the content and conduct of the program has been described previously (Dugan-Jendzejec, 1982).

Instrumentation

Four instruments were used in conducting this study. One aspect of psychological health was recorded by the Bradburn's (1969) Affect Balance Scale (ABS). This multidimensional, objective scale basically assesses feelings of happiness towards one's current state of affairs. The rationale for choosing the ABS over some measure of life satisfaction and morale is that it emphasizes affect, a short time-frame referent, and the transitory moods of gaiety or pleasure whereas life satisfaction and morale measures have cognitive connotations, an orientation to life as a whole, and are relatively stable or fixed (George & Bearon, 1980). Other reasons for using the ABS are that it is comprised of a short number of items and is easily administered to older subjects (George & Bearon, 1980). The ABS has been correlated with the Life Satisfaction Instrument A Scale (r = .66), the Rosow Moral Scale (r = .61), and a nine-item mental illness scale (r = .64). Test-retest reliability for the instrument has been reported as .76. The Cronbach item alpha for the groups used in this study were .51 (based on posttest data).

The ABS consists of 10 items that requires either a "yes" or "no" response. Five items comprise the Positive Affect Scale and five items make up the Negative Affect Scale. For both subscales every "yes" response received 1 point, and every "no" response received 0 points. As the developer of the ABS suggests, a global psychological well-being score was calculated by subtracting the sum of the negative items (ranging from 0 to 5 points) from the sum of the positive items (ranging from 0 to 5 points) and adding a constant of 5 points. The theoretical range of scores for the ABS thus could be 0 to 10, with a higher score reflecting more positive psychological well-being.

Another aspect of psychological health that was measured in the study was self-concept. Self-concept is the cognitive component of the self and consists of the individual's judgment of what he/she is really like. Self-concept was measured by self-report to a single-item question. The rationale for operationalizing self-concept this way was to take a different approach than was used for measuring affect—namely a subjective, unidimensional approach. Furthermore, such an operationalized measure of self-concept is deemed as having face validity, being easy to administer, and being less likely to elicit respondent fatigue (Gaitz & Scott, 1972; George & Bearon, 1980).

For this study, self-concept was gauged by the question, "How do you feel about yourself as a person?" The response possibilities to the question were scored as follows: a "pretty good" response received 4 points; a "just okay," 3 points; a "could be better," 2 points; and a "not so good," 1 point.

Based on a face validity approach, verbal interaction was measured by using a version of the collective typology proposed by Bales (1950). More specifically, a total verbal interaction score was calculated (using a checklist approach in data collection) for each participant in the experimental group by adding the number of observed verbal contacts of an initiating nature with another person (such as asking for an orientation, an opinion, or a suggestion) to the number of a observed verbal contacts of a responding nature with another person (e.g., giving an opinion or orientation). Interactions with a fellow participant, a music therapist, or the observer were recorded. The total number of verbal interactions recorded for the experimental group during the first six sessions was compared to the total number of verbal interactions registered for this group during the last six music sessions.

By and large, face validity was used for developing questions covering demographic characteristics. Institutional records were consulted to ascertain a study participant's age and length of institutionalization. Members of the study were asked to assess their health by responding to a single-item subjective health rating that has been used in previous studies. Significant correlations have been reported between subjective health ratings and physicians' ratings as well as between subjective health ratings and a variety of other health related variables (George & Bearon, 1980). Test-retest correlations for a single-item measure of health have ranged from .32 to .71 (George & Bearon, 1980). During pretest data collection the question posed to respondents in the study was, "Overall, how would you rate your physical health?" Response categories provided were "excellent," "good," "fair," and "poor."

Additionally, individuals were queried regarding their music appreciation. Based on face validity, a Music Appreciation Index was constructed from the responses given to three questions: (1) "Did you take music courses in college?"; (2) "Do you/have you played a musical instrument?"; and (3) "Do you enjoy concerts, operas, musicals, and the like?" For each "yes" response 1 point was recorded and for each "no" response 0 points were recorded. Thus, the scores for the Index ranged from 0 points to 3 points. An individual was deemed as having high music appreciation if the score was 2 points or greater; conversely, an individual was considered to have low music appreciation if the score was 1 point or less. Lastly, respondents were queried about their involvement in previous nursing home-sponsored music programs. Based on face validity this concept was operationalized by the question, "Have you participated in music programs previously offered at this nursing home?" Possible answers were "yes" or "no."

Collection of Data

Instruments used in the study were piloted with 5 residents of a nursing home (one that was not used for either the experimental or control group nursing home), and no problems in administering the measures emerged. In the privacy of their rooms, pilot and study participants were asked the questions contained in the various instruments by one of the investigators. Questions dealing with demographic characteristics of the study participant were posed at the pretest data collection phase. On the average, it took about 30 minutes to respond to the questions being posed. In order to monitor verbal interaction, the second author was present at all the music sessions.

Statistics

Hypotheses testing was done using one-tailed probability. Given the small sample size, a probability of $\leq .30$ was adopted. As Labovitz (1968) has pointed out, the power of the test varies directly with sample size. With a larger sample size a small difference is likely to be statistically significant, whereas with a small sample size even large differences may not reach the predetermined level. Statistical analyses were performed with the University of Maryland's Sperry-Univac 1100/82 Computer System. The Statistical Package for Social Sciences was used for the statistical calculations (Nie, Hull, Jenkins, Steinbrenner, & Bent, 1975).

RESULTS

Demographic characteristics of the individuals involved in the study are presented in Table 1. Essentially the two groups were evenly matched in terms of gender (a majority of the individ-

TABLE 1
Demographic Characteristics of Experimental and Control Group Members

Characteristic	Group: Experimental (n = 10)	Group: Control (n = 14)
	%	
Gender		
Male	30.0	21.4
Female	70.0	78.6
Age		
60–88	50.0	51.1
89–97	50.0	48.9
Length of institutionalization		
Two years or less	60.0	50.0
More than two years	40.0	50.0
Self-perceived health		
Excellent-good	60.0	71.4
Fair-poor	40.0	28.6
Music appreciation index		
High	40.0	64.3
Low	60.0	35.7
Previous music program experience		
Yes	50.0	0.0
No	50.0	100.0

uals in both groups were female), age (about one half of the individuals in both groups were 88 or younger, and about one half were 89 or older), length of institutionalization (60% of the experimental group compared to 50% of the control group had lived in the nursing home 2 years or less), and health status (60% compared to approximately 70% of the experimental and control groups, respectively, labeled self in good to excellent health).

Differences did exist between the two groups in regard to music appreciation and previous participation in music programs in their facility. That is, the majority of experimental group had low music appreciation scores, whereas a majority of the control group scored high in music appreciation. In respect to past music program involvement, one half of the experimental group compared to none of the control group reported participating in music-related programs since living in their respective facilities.

The first step in the analysis was to ascertain preintervention equivalency between the experimental and control groups on affect balance and self-concept. Nonsignificant *t* values for affect balance, $t(22) = .52$, $p = .61$, and self concept, $t(22) = 1.33$, $p = .20$, indicated that the groups were evenly matched.

Both the experimental group (*M* pretest = 5.40, *M* posttest = 5.80) and the control group (*M* pretest = 4.93, *M* posttest = 5.00) underwent a shift in their affect balance. Moreover, the difference in the amount of change between the two groups was significant, $F(1,22) = .19$, $p = .18$. Contrastingly, for self concept, a between group comparison on mean change (experimental group's *M* pretest = 3.10 and *M* posttest = 3.10 versus control group's *M* pretest = 2.57 and *M* posttest = 3.00) was not significant, $F(1,22) = .12$, $p = .37$.

Examination of the verbal interactions of the experimental group over the course of the music sessions (first 6 sessions *M* = 39.14, last 6 sessions *M* = 71.60) revealed a substantial increase in the amount of verbal interaction among the music participants. A statistically significant, $t(8) = 3.14$, $p = .00$, change occurred in the total number of verbal interactions observed in the first half of the music program when compared to the last half of the program.

DISCUSSION

At the very least, the music program offered had an appreciable and sizable impact on the affect balance and verbal interactions of the treatment group over a period of time. As such these findings, in part, both support (Cassity, 1976; Meseck, 1978; Reigler, 1980) and contradict (Phillips, 1980; Wolfe, 1983) results noted in earlier studies. It should be pointed out, however, that both groups' ABS scores deviated considerably from what has been observed in normal populations. That is, the mean ABS for a normal sample has been reported as 8.17, and the mean for a psychiatric sample has been noted as 4.25 (George & Bearon, 1980). All this suggests that special efforts may be needed to improve the quality of life of nursing home residents.

The increase in spontaneous dialogue may be explained by the Hawthorne effect, that is, the observer's presence rather than the music program was responsible for the change in social or verbal interaction. Another plausible explanation may be that the increase in verbal interaction occurred because, with the passage of time, the group became more comfortable with their fellow participants, the instructors, and the music program. This conjecture is supported by the results of a separate analysis of the nature of verbal interaction changes. It was found that the average number of initiating interactions increased, whereas the number of responding interactions remained more or less constant. Examples of initiating interactions that were observed were that the participants became less hesitant to ask questions about the music material presented, and, on more than one occasion, individual group members discovered that someone else appreciated their favorite song or type of music.

The results provide impetus for further investigations. Other rigorous studies are needed on how involvement by nursing home residents in music programs affects their sensory functioning, music appreciation, self-perceived creativity, and/or boredom reduction. Somewhat related is the issue of how variations in frequency and intensity of music programs impact on the health of nursing home residents. Another topic for study is to assess how participation in a music program affects self-concept when using an instrument more sophisticated in terms of validity and reliability. Still another area for research is to examine whether nursing home residents with special backgrounds (e.g., individuals who have high regard or appreciation for music and have not had the opportunity to participate in a music program) glean more from a music program. Lastly, it is important to understand whether or not there are any long-term or carry-over effects of music program participation.

In summary, further research studies using quasi-experimental designs that control for extraneous factors are needed in order to answer the following questions: Do music programs work? How can they be improved? It is still not clear how and under what circumstances music programs emerge as therapeutic tools for working with institutionalized elders. Regardless, it seems warranted to advocate the creation and continuation of music programs at the institutional level.

ACKNOWLEDGEMENTS

This research was supported in part by a Social and Behavioral Research Support Award from the University of Maryland's College of Physical Education, Recreation, and Health and the University of Maryland's Computation Center. Appreciation is extended to Anne Lipe, RMT, who critically reviewed an earlier draft of this manuscript.

REFERENCES

Atchley, R. (1977). *The social forces in later life.* Belmont, CA: Wadsworth Publishing Co.

Bales, R. (1950). *Interaction process analysis: A method for the study of small groups.* Cambridge, MA: Addison-Wesley.

Bradburn, N. (1969). *The structure of psychological well-being.* Chicago: Aldine Publishing Co.

Bright, R. (1972). *Music in geriatric care.* New York: St. Martin's Press.

Burnside, I. (Ed.) (1978). *Working with the elderly: Group processes and techniques.* Belmont, CA: Duxbury Press.

Cassity, M. (1976). The influence of a music therapy activity upon peer acceptance, group cohesiveness, and interpersonal relationships of adult psychiatric patients. *Journal of Music Therapy, 2,* 66–76.

Douglass, D. (1978). *Happiness is music, music, music.* Salem, OR: LaRoux Enterprises.

Dugan-Jendzejec, M. (1982). *The effects of a music therapy program on nursing home residents.* Unpublished Master's thesis, University of Maryland, College Park.

Gaitz, C., & Scott, J. (1972). Age and the measurement of mental health. *Journal of Health and Social Behavior, 13,* 55–67.

Gaston, E. (1968). *Music in Therapy.* New York: Macmillan Publishing Co.

George, L., & Bearon, L. (1980). *Quality of life in older persons: Meaning and measurement.* New York: Human Sciences Press, Inc.

Hennessey, M. (1978). Music and music therapy groups. In I. Burnside (Ed.), *Working with the elderly: Group Processes and Techniques* (pp. 255–274). Belmont, CA: Duxbury Press.

Labovitz, S. (1968). Criteria for selecting a significance test: A note on the sacredness of .05. *The American Sociologist, 3,* 220–222.

Meseck, K. (1978). An evaluation of music therapy with geriatric patients. *Canadian Music Therapy Journal, 6,* 7–13.

Nie, N., Hull, C. Jenkins, J., Steinbrenner, K., & Bent, D. (1975). *Statistical package for the social sciences.* New York: McGraw-Hill.

Phillips, J. (1980). Music in nursing of elderly persons in nursing homes. *Gerontological Nursing, 6,* 37–39.

Reigler, J. (1980). Comparison of a reality orientation program for geriatric patients with and without music. *Journal of Music Therapy, 1,* 26–33.

Tanner, D., & O'Briant, R. (1980). Music can color a graying America. *Music Educators Journal, 4,* 28–31.

Wolfe, J. (1983). The use of music in a group sensory training program for regressed geriatric patients. *Activities, Adaptation & Aging*, *4*, 49–62.

14

INTERGENERATIONAL RECREATION: EFFECTS ON ATTITUDES AND VISUAL PROXEMIC BEHAVIORS

Paul S. Miko

Sixty college students participated in selected recreational activities with either robust elderly, frail elderly, or student peers in an experimental investigation of potential attitudinal and behavioral effects of intergenerational recreation. Self-reported attitudes appeared unaffected, while nonreactive videotape recordings indicated significant group differences in visual proxemic interactions.

> Old age is like any other stage of life—it has both positive and negative features, but stereotypes prevent us from seeing aging in a realistic manner. —(Gene Ezell, 1982, p. 40)

Currently there are 10 million undergraduate students between 14 and 34 years of age attending American colleges and universities (U. S. Bureau of the Census, 1980). In their various roles as future policy makers, social planners, business executives, human service providers, etc., these students will have a significant impact on the quality of life of all older Americans. It is important that their attitudes and behaviors toward the elderly are based on objective knowledge and experience and not on stereotypical misconceptions.

Over 30 years of research on college students' attitudes and behaviors toward old people has revealed the following:

- Negative attitudes and stereotypes with respect to old age and old people appear to be widespread among college students (Kogan, 1961; Palmore, 1980; Tuckman & Lorge, 1953.
- Certain intergenerational experiences or situational contexts appear to positively influence college students' attitudes toward old people (Crockett, Press, & Osterkamp, 1979; Naus, 1973; Sherman, Gold, & Sherman, 1978).
- Certain intergenerational experiences or situational contexts appear to negatively influence college students' attitudes toward old people (Auerback & Levenson, 1977; Rosencranz & McNevin, 1969).
- The multidimensionality of attitudes and behaviors of college students toward old people underscores the need for multi-dimensional investigative methodologies (Green, 1981; McTavish, 1971; Weinberger & Milham, 1975).

The present study was a multidimensional examination of various effects of intergenerational contact within the specific situational context of intergenerational recreation. The research objective was to determine experimentally the influence of intergenerational participation in selected recreational activities with either robust elderly or frail elderly individuals on undergraduate students' attitudes toward old people and on visual proxemic behaviors (i.e., interpersonal, biocommunicative, and usually subconscious eye movements). The overall purpose of the study was to better understand the potential role of intergenerational recreation in minimizing stereotypical misconceptions that "prevent us from seeing aging in a realistic manner."

METHODS

Sixty undergraduate student volunteers (44 males, 16 females, mean age = 22) from various academic majors were randomly assigned to participate in 1 hour of selected recreational activities with robust elderly, frail elderly, or undergraduate-age peers. The "recreational activities" were a set format of 10 interactional games based on the New Games Foundation philosophy of creative and cooperative play (Fluegelman, 1976). The "robust elderly" were 12 volunteers (5 males, 7 females, mean age = 66) who were enrolled in a vigorous senior citizen physical fitness program at a nearby community college; the "frail elderly" were 8 volunteers (3 males, 5 females, mean age = 76) who were members of a senior day care program and in need of supportive services due to continuing physical and/or psychological disability. During the recreational activities, visual proxemic interactions were videotape recorded. After the recreational activities, the 60 student subjects were asked to complete Kogan's Old People Scale (Kogan, 1961).

Sex, frequency of involvement with old people, and socioeconomic level of parents were identified as major confounding variables. Chi-square tests on descriptive data provided by the student subjects were used to determine if random assignment of subjects and treatments had counterbalanced group differences on these three variables.

To determine if attitudes toward old people varied as a result of participation in the recreational activities with either robust elderly, frail elderly, or undergraduate peers, Bartlett's tests for homogeneity of variance followed by fixed-effects, one-way analyses of variance were performed on the student subjects' positive and negative mean scores on Kogan's Old People Scale. Kogan's Old People Scale was initially chosen for use in this study because of its proven reliability and validity (Shaw & Wright, 1967) as well as its reported ability to predict a subject's "disposition to associate with the aged" (Silverman, 1966, p. 87). With regard to reliability, Kogan (1961) computed odd-even reliabilities for the OP+ and OP– scales separately using three groups of college students with *n*'s of 128, 186, and 168. Corrected reliabilities were .66, .73, and .77, for the OP+ scale and .73, .83, and .76 for the OP– scale respectively.

To determine if there were significant differences in visual proxemic behaviors, the three videotape recordings of student subjects participating in recreational activities with either robust elderly, frail elderly, or undergraduate peers were subsequently viewed by 42 undergraduate volunteers who were not involved in the initial activity treatment groups. Prior to the actual data collection, these 42 students participated in a researcher-led basic training session on the techniques of visual proxemic behavior notation based on recommendations by Hall (1974). The training consisted of reviewing black and white 35 mm photos illustrating the various behavior categories comprising Hall's Eye Behavior Scale. This was followed by practice ratings of dyadic visual proxemic behaviors on videotape recordings. The main objective of the training was to develop among the undergraduate student raters a basic understanding of and accommodation to Hall's Eye Behavior Scale. The racial differences among the undergraduate student raters precluded any attempt at establishing generalized interrater reliability coefficients since both eye behavior as well as eye behavior ratings vary greatly from race to race. To minimize this inherent limitation, a counterbalanced Latin square design with random assignment of raters to groups and random selection of independent Latin squares was employed in the collection of the group visual proxemic behavior ratings. Chi-square tests were then used to analyze and compare the frequencies of categorical ratings received by each activity treatment group on the Eye Behavior Scale.

FINDINGS

Chi-square tests on sex, frequency of involvement with old people, and socioeconomic levels of parents indicated that there were no significant group differences at the $p < .05$ level among the student subjects participating in either the robust elderly, frail elderly, or undergraduate peer activity treatment groups. Random assignment of subjects to groups and treatments successfully counterbalanced individual subject anomalies on these three potentially confounding variables. The descriptive data on total frequency of involvement with the old people provided by the students was of special interest in that it indicated that the category of "all of the time" received an average of only 4.0 percent of the total number of responses while the category "never" received 32.9 percent.

Bartlett's tests and one-way analyses of variance indicated that there were no significant group differences at the $p < .05$ level among the students' positive and negative mean scores on Kogan's Old People Scale after participation in recreational acitivities with either robust elderly, frail elderly, or undergraduate peers. Although not statistically significant at the $p < .05$ level, it was nevertheless noted that the undergraduate students who had participated in the recreational activities with the frail elderly had, as a group, the highest mean positive attitudinal score and the lowest mean negative attitudinal score of all three recreational activity treatment groups. See Table 1.

Chi-square tests on the frequencies of categorical ratings re-

TABLE 1
Student Subjects' Frequency of Involvement with Old People and Mean Scores on Kogan's Old People Scale[a]

Groups	Undergraduates–Robust elderly	Undergraduates–Frail elderly	Undergraduates–Undergraduates
Frequency of *involvement*:			
All of the time	3.2%	4.1%	4.7%
Most of the time	10.3%	21.8%	17.7%
Some of the time	48.4%	48.9%	42.2%
Never	38.1%	25.2%	35.4%
Old People Positive Mean scores:	4.35	4.37	4.11
Old People Negative Mean scores:	2.43	2.40	2.57

[a]Kogan's Old People Scale consists of 17 matched positive-negative pairs of statements. A score of 3.5 indicates attitudinal neutrality.

ceived by each recreational activity treatment group on Hall's Eye Behavior Scale indicated no statistically significant differences at the $p < .05$ level between the undergraduate–robust elderly and undergraduate–undergraduate groups. However, chi-square tests did indicate statistically significant differences at the $p < .001$ level between the undergraduate–frail elderly group and both the undergraduate–robust elderly and undergraduate–undergraduate groups. A further analysis of the incidence of visual contact in terms of individual group categorical percentages indicated that the undergraduate–robust elderly and undergraduate–undergraduate groups each received 33 percent of their total visual proxemic behavior ratings in the high incidence of visual contact categories, whereas the undergraduate–frail elderly group received 42.9 percent of its ratings in the high incidence of visual contact categories. See Table 2.

DISCUSSION

The present study confirmed the implicit need for increased intergenerational interaction. Less than one twentieth of the total

TABLE 2
Group Visual Proxemic Behavior Ratings

Groups	Undergraduates–Robust elderly	Undergraduates–Frail elderly*	Undergraduates–Undergraduates
Incidence of Visual Contact:			
High	424 (31.3%)	544 (42.9%)	435 (33.3%)
Medium	500 (39.0%)	412 (32.5%)	523 (40.0%)
Low	358 (27.9%)	312 (24.6%)	349 (26.7%)

*Significant at $p < .001$

number of responses to the frequency of involvement with old people were in the "all of the time" category while almost one third were in the "never" category. The students who provided the frequency of involvement data were from various academic majors including nursing, business, engineering, architecture, government, journalism, law enforcement, and computer science. It is not unreasonable to assume that many of these students in the near future will be involved in decision-making processes which will have an impact on the lives of old people. It is unfortunate that so many of these students indicated so little experientially oriented intergenerational involvement to assist them in "seeing aging in a realistic manner."

A second finding of this study, with particular implications for recreation programmers, was the absence of any significant negative effects on the undergraduate students' attitudes toward old people as a result of participation in intergenerational recreation with either robust or frail elderly. Auerbach and Levenson (1977) and Rosencranz and McNevin (1969) reported that certain situational contexts might negatively influence college students' attitudes toward old people. The results of this study indicated that the situational context of intergenerational participation in cooperative recreational activities with either robust or frail elderly had no significant negative effects on the college students' attitudes toward old people. In other words, none of the results of this experimental study in any way contraindicate the planning of or participation in similar intergenerational recreation programs.

Too often recreation programming is characterized by age as well as disability segregation. The results of this study support neither type of programming. On the contrary, the fact that the students in the undergraduate–frail elderly treatment group exhibited the highest mean group positive and lowest mean group negative attitudinal scores could be interpreted to indicate that similar age- and disability-integrated recreation programs (especially similar programs lasting longer than the 1 hour limit used in this study) might be potentially beneficial with regard to college students' attitudes toward old people. At the very least, similar recreation programs for college students and robust or frail elderly would provide a greater opportunity for creative, cooperative, and ultimately enjoyable intergenerational interaction.

A third finding of this study was the influence that underraduate–frail elderly participation in the selected recreational activities appeared to have on visual proxemic behaviors. The undergraduate–frail elderly group was perceived as engaging in significantly different visual proxemic behaviors than either the undergraduate–robust elderly or undergraduate–undergraduate groups. This difference among the activity treatment groups was most pronounced in the higher incidence of direct eye-to-eye-/face-to-face interactions that occurred in the undergraduate–frail elderly group. Argyle and Dean (1965) noted, "Without eye contact, people do not feel that they are fully in communication" (p. 289). The higher incidence of eye contact exhibited by the undergraduates and frail elderly may very well have been indicative of their being more "fully in communication."

Mehrabian (1972) examined the findings of Exline (1963), Exline and Eldridge (1965), Exline, Gray, and Schuette (1965), Mehrabian (1969), and Nachshon and Wapner (1967) and concluded that "more eye contact of communicators is typically associated with more positive attitudes between them" (p. 22). If the higher incidence of visual contact within the undergraduate–frail elderly group is interpreted as being associated with positive interpersonal attitudes, then there is further reason to advocate age- and disability-intergrated recreational programs of this type. Potentially beneficial experiences can result from having college students participate in cooperative recreational activities with frail elderly individuals, namely, a greater opportunity for intergenerational interaction and interpersonal communication and the increased possibility of positive attitudinal sharing.

Finally, the need for multidimensional investigative methodologies in attitudinal research recommended by Green (1981) and McTavish (1971) was underscored by the results of this study. The use of self-reported descriptive and attitudinal questionnaires in conjunction with nonreactive videotape recordings and observer-assigned behavior ratings permitted a more in-depth and informative analysis than would have been possible if these investigative techniques had been employed separately. Also, when considered collectively, the multiple findings of this study concerning the low freqency of intergenerational involvement, the absence of adverse attitudinal treatment effects, and the high incidence of visual interaction among the undergraduates and the frail elderly participants, combined to illustrate more clearly the potentially beneficial role cooperative intergenerational recreation can play in the enhancement of communication and understanding between college students and old people.

> If Freud said that the child is father to the man, then it may also be said that the man always retains a bit of the child. For when the young and old play and learn together, they have mutual respect and affection.
>
> (Leviton and Campanelli, 1982, p. 6)

REFERENCES

Argyle, M., & Dean, J. (1965). Eye-contact, distance and affiliation. *Sociometry, 28*, 289–304.

Auerbach, D. H., & Levinson, R. L., Jr. (1977). Second impressions: Attitude change in college students toward the elderly. *Gerontologist, 17*, 362–366.

Crocket, W. H., Press, A. N., & Osterkamp, M. (1979).The effect of deviations from stereotyped expectations upon attitudes toward older persons. *Journal of Gerontology, 34*, 369–374.

Exline, R. V., (1963). Explorations in the process of perception: Visual interaction in relation to competition, sex, and need for affiliation, *Journal of Personality, 31*, 1–20.

Exline, R. V., & Eldridge, C., (1987). Effects of two patterns of a speaker's visual behavior upon the perception of the authenticity of his verbal message. Paper presented at the meeting of the Eastern Psychological Association, Boston, April, 1967.

Exline, R. V., Gray, D., & Schuette, D. (1965). Visual behavior in a dyad as affected by interview content and sex of respondent. *Journal of Personality and Social Psychology, 1*. 201–209.

Ezell, G. (1982). Youth's image of the elderly. *Health Education, 13,* (2), 40–41.

Fleugelman, A. (Ed.) (1976). *The new games book.* San Francisco: Headlands Press.

Green, S. K. (1981). Attitudes and perceptions about the elderly: Current and future perspectives. *International Journal of Aging and Human Development, 13,* 99–119.

Hall, E. T. (1974). *Handbook for proxemic research.* Washington, DC: Society for the Anthropology of Visual Communication.

Kogan, N. (1961). Attitudes toward old people: The development of a scale and an examination of correlates. *Journal of Abnormal and Social Psychology, 62,* 44–54.

Leviton, D., & Campanelli, L. (1982). HPERD for two forgotten populations—"the frail aged" and "dying aged": Challenge and response. *The Easterner, 7* (1), 1, 3, 5–6.

Mehrabian, A., (1969). Methods & designs: Some referents and measures of nonverbal behavior. *Behavior Research Methods and Instrumentation, 1,* 203–207.

Mehrabian, A. (1972). *Nonverbal communication.* New York: Atherton.

McTavish, D. G., (1971). Perceptions of old people: A review of research methodologies and findings. *Gerontologist, 11,* 90–101.

Nachshon, I., & Wapner, S., (1967). Effect of eye contact and physiognomy on perceived location of other person. *Journal of Personality and Social Psychology, 7,* 82–89.

Naus, P. J. (1973). Some correlates of attitudes towards old people. *International Journal of Aging and Human Development, 4,* 229–243.

Palmore, E., (1980). The facts on aging quiz: A review of findings. *Gerontologist, 20,* 669–672.

Rosencranz, H. A., & McNevin, T. E. (1969). A factor analysis of attitudes toward the aged. *Gerontologist, 9,* 55–59.

Shaw, M. E., & Wright, J. M. (1967). *Scales for the measurement of attitudes.* New York: McGraw-Hill.

Sherman, N. C., Gold, J. A., & Sherman, M. F. (1978). Attribution theory and evaluations of older men among college students, their parents, and grandparents. *Personality and Social Psychology Bulletin, 4,* 440–442.

Silverman, I. (1966). Response-set bias and predictive validity associated with Kogan's "Attitudes toward old people scale." *Journal of Gerontology, 21,* 86–88.

Tuckman, J., & Lorge, I. (1953). Attitudes toward old people. *Journal of Social Psychology, 37,* 249–260.

U. S. Bureau of the Census. (1980). School enrollment-social and economic characteristics of students: October 1980 (advance report). *Current Population Reports,* Series P-20, No. 362. Washington, DC.

Weinberger, L. E., & Millham, J. (1975). A multi-dimensional, multiple method analysis of attitudes toward the elderly. *Journal of Gerontology, 30,* 343–348.

INDEX